Antibias Regulation of Universities

Antibias Regulation of Universities

FACULTY PROBLEMS AND THEIR SOLUTIONS

by Richard A. Lester

Professor of Economics
Princeton University

A Report Prepared for
The Carnegie Commission on Higher Education

MCGRAW-HILL BOOK COMPANY

New York St. Louis San Francisco Düsseldorf
London Sydney Toronto Mexico Panama
Johannesburg Kuala Lumpur Montreal
New Delhi São Paulo Singapore

The Carnegie Commission on Higher Education, 2150 Shattuck Avenue, Berkeley, California 94704, has sponsored preparation of this report as part of a continuing effort to obtain and present significant information for public discussion. The views expressed are those of the author.

ANTIBIAS REGULATION OF UNIVERSITIES
Faculty Problems and Their Solutions

This book was set in Vladimir by University Graphics, Inc. It was printed and bound by The Whitlock Press, Inc. The designers were Elliot Epstein and Edward Butler. The editors were Nancy Tressel and Michael Hennelly for McGraw-Hill Book Company and Verne A. Stadtman for the Carnegie Commission on Higher Education. Milton J. Heiberg supervised the production.

Library of Congress Cataloging in Publication Data

Lester, Richard Allen, date
Antibias regulation of universities.

Bibliography: p.
1. Universities and colleges—United States—Faculty. 2. Faculty integration—United States.
I. Carnegie Commission on Higher Education. II. Title
III. Faculty problems and their solutions.

LB2331.7.L47 331.7′61′378120973 74-6422
ISBN 0-07-010120-5

123456789WHWH7987654

Contents

Foreword

The Carnegie Commission on Higher Education has consistently expressed support for efforts to increase the relative participation of women and members of minority groups in college and university faculties. It has recognized, however, that such efforts will be accomplished with considerable difficulty and probably more slowly than we might wish.

In our report entitled *Opportunities for Women in Higher Education,* and in a technical note to our final report *Priorities for Action,* we reviewed some actions that must be taken if the difficulties are to be overcome. Among them are increasing the numbers of women and members of minorities who pursue graduate studies and become part of the "pool" of qualified academic talent available for faculty appointment; finding jobs for new faculty members during a period in which little or no enrollment growth is anticipated and existing faculties are well staffed by relatively young men and women; and matching new faculty members who seek jobs with the often highly specialized openings that may occur.

Some of these same problems have been of concern to Richard A. Lester, who has conducted an extended independent study of the issues involved and has had practical experience with employment practices and compensation differentials in both industry and academe. He has served as chairman of the Southern Textile Commission under the National War Labor Board (1945), as vice-chairman of the President's Commission on the Status of Women (1961–1963), Dean of the Faculty of Princeton University (1968–1973), and chairman of Princeton's Equal Employment Opportunity Committee (1968–1972).

In this book, Lester reports on his studies and discusses many of the specific problems associated with increasing the membership of women and members of minority groups on the faculties of major colleges and universities. He stresses the fact that current faculty members favor such an increase, but warns that many of the action programs prescribed to achieve it fail to take into consideration either the inadequate supply of qualified people among those groups currently underrepresented on our faculties or the characteristics of academic employment that distinguish it from employment in industry. At stake is not only an equitable system of academic employment, but also loss of financial support as governments apply economic sanctions to achieve numerical hiring goals that often have little relevance to the character and mission of universities. Lester has given us a sensible and well-documented study that should be vitally important as our colleges, universities, and state and federal governments consider or reconsider the policies that guide them in this difficult and sensitive area. He speaks with the authority of a person with extensive and most successful experience in the field of industrial relations and academic administration and with the credentials of a long-time supporter of equal opportunity. His wisdom and his advice merit the most careful consideration.

Clark Kerr
Chairman
Carnegie Commission
on Higher Education

May 1974

Preface

Since 1968, universities and colleges having federal research contracts have been under antibias regulation by the federal government. The regulation, enforced by the Department of Health, Education, and Welfare, has been unsatisfactory in certain respects to various parties—university faculty and administrators, interested women and men in academic communities, and persons in concerned organizations and in government.

Difficulties were to be expected in the first five years of a program that involves such a sensitive and complex subject as discrimination in faculty employment in universities and colleges. The question to ask is: How much have we learned from five years of experience, and is the program generating difficulties and ill-effects unnecessary for the achievement of its legitimate purposes? This book attempts to answer that question and, in doing so, proposes some different solutions to the problems involved.

In presenting criticisms of government programs, and proposing alternative ways to achieve and enforce nondiscrimination for university faculties, I do so out of a strong conviction that prejudice in employment, on account of race, sex, religion, or other nonperformance factors, is destructive of democratic values and violates the principle of appointment and promotion on merit, which is so vital for achievement of the educational objectives of our institutions of higher learning. It should also be said that some of the criticisms and proposals in the book were presented to HEW officials by me in January 1972, in September 1972, and in October and December 1973.

Some of the ideas offered here have much wider application than just to the faculties of universities. I leave it to those versed in other areas of activity to develop such broader applications.

The writing of this book was my own idea, and the product is mine. I have purposely avoided seeking financial support for the project. The Carnegie Commission on Higher Education has no responsibility for any opinion and bias in these pages.

Many persons have helped to sharpen the reasoning and improve the ideas and analysis in this book. They have done so through discussion of views and experience and by reading parts of the first draft of the manuscript and giving me the benefit of their criticisms and suggestions. I particularly wish to express my appreciation to the following for their contribution, but hasten to add that none of them is responsible for the particular views or proposals presented in the book: Robert L. Aronson, Orley Ashenfelter, William G. Bowen, J. Douglas Brown, John H. Bunzel, Robert R. France, Marjorie Galenson, Eli Ginzberg, Frederick H. Harbison, Clark Kerr, William F. Miller, Charles A. Myers, Robert B. McKersie, Albert Rees, Adele Simmons, Sheldon Steinbach, Phyllis Wallace, Edwin H. Young, and Verne A. Stadtman, whose skillful editing has greatly improved the book's readability.

The staff of the Industrial Relations Section of Princeton University—Helen E. Fairbanks, Dorothy Silvester, Karen Stout, and Irene Rowe—have been of valuable assistance in a variety of ways, including preparation of the manuscript for the press.

Richard A. Lester
Princeton, New Jersey

Antibias Regulation of Universities

1. *Introduction*

Equal opportunity for each person to rise to the top—as a student and as a faculty member—on the basis of individual merit, is essential for the healthy functioning of institutions of advanced learning. Painful experience in this country and abroad has demonstrated the corrosive effects on the creation and cultivation of truth when outside groups—government, business, religious, or other special interests—exert too much pressure or gain significant control over the operation of universities. The professional integrity of the search for, and distribution of, truth must be maintained if the intellectual leadership in a country is to be free from the bonds of prejudice.

THE NATURE OF OUR INQUIRY

The problem of eliminating bias in the appointment, advancement, and compensation of faculty of major universities—without hampering their professional purposes or their potential for benefiting mankind—is presented in this book. That is a complex problem with many ramifications. Analysis of the problem's various facets involves critical examination of government programs that enforce "affirmative action" against job discrimination as applied to the faculties of the most advanced universities. We shall examine the implications that "compliance" with federal and state antibias programs may have on the future of our distinguished institutions of higher education over, say, the next 30 years, which is about the average length of faculty tenure appointments by promotion.

Our analysis will draw on experience, especially since 1968, in particular institutions. Our analysis should not, however, be considered a report of individual case studies. During 1973 and early 1974, discussions of problems and experiences were held with administrators and faculty members at some 20 universities across the country, with compliance officials in Washington and in several regional offices of the Department of Health, Education, and Welfare (HEW), and with staff personnel in associations of colleges and universities. No direct quotations are, however, presented from such conversations. Frankness was encouraged by assurance that the specifics of those discussions would be used primarily for understanding problems and developing possible solutions for them. Therefore, only published material is used in reference to individual institutions or persons.

University faculty and administrators generally are sympathetic with the elimination of prejudice from faculty employment, whether based on race, sex, religion, ethnic origin, or any other grounds. Indeed, many of them could be considered oversympathetic. For instance, a broad national survey shows that about 32 percent of the male and 42 percent of the female faculty of universities questioned in the 1972–73 academic year favored preferential hiring for women in faculty positions at their institutions. Preferential hiring for members of minority groups was favored by 35 percent of the male faculty and 36 percent of the female faculty.[1] Faculty members want to avoid being labeled as "prejudiced" against blacks, women, or persons with particular religious views, or being charged with violating particular antidiscrimination legislation or federal executive orders banning bias in employment.

Although university faculty are quite individualistic and mixed in their positions on particular issues, numerous surveys have shown that a high proportion of university professors are liberal or left of center in their social and political views (see Ladd & Lipset, 1973, pp. 16, 18–19, 22–26, 28). However, they tend to be relatively conservative or cautious concerning change in internal university operations. Also, in each age group, the distinguished, highly achieving professors in the prestigious institutions generally are disproportionately more liberal—"display the greatest inclination to support politics of social criticism from perspectives of egalitarian and popular values"—than are professors in the middle-tier and lower-tier institutions (ibid., pp. 19, 22–27).

On the issue of race and sex bias, and affirmative action to achieve government-specified, numerical hiring goals for women

[1] The percentages are significantly smaller for two-year colleges. In those institutions, male faculty figures were 20 percent favoring preferential hiring for women and 28 percent for members of minorities. See Bayer (1973, p. 30). In a 1968–69 survey with approximately the same coverage, 23 percent of the men and 20 percent of the women on university faculties favored "relaxing" the normal academic requirements in appointing "members of minority groups" to positions on their faculty. See Bayer (1970, p. 17).

and blacks in universities and elsewhere in the economy, university professors often find themselves somewhat torn by conflicting philosophic viewpoints. Some, especially in the social sciences and the humanities (ibid., p. 28), may favor action beyond equal opportunity extending into equality of results. But they and their colleagues may also be quite concerned about assaults on the principle of selection and reward according to individual merit, in the economy in general and in university faculties in particular.[2]

Generally speaking, university faculty and top university administrators can be expected to support appointment, advancement, and compensation of individual faculty members on the basis of merit, judged by past performance and by future promise as indicated by previous experience. On educational as well as legal and moral grounds, they can be expected to want to conform to the principle of equal opportunity for faculty employment for all qualified persons. It may, however, be difficult to convince all concerned, including some students, advocacy groups, and compliance officers, that the best-qualified candidate for a particular position was appointed or promoted to tenure from among the candidates who emerge in open competition. Differences of opinion may arise on the qualities that a particular university most needs in its faculty, in general and especially for a particular opening. Differences may also involve which candidate's abilities and potential as a teacher-scholar best fit an ideal conception of the position.

LEGAL BASIS FOR GOVERNMENT CONTROL

Executive Order No. 11246, approved by President Lyndon B. Johnson in September 1965, provides that as a condition of obtaining federal contracts, all contractors, including universities with research contracts, sign an agreement not to "discriminate against any employee or applicant for employment because of race, color, religion, or national origin." Sex was added to that list by Executive Order No. 11375, effective October 1968. The Department of Labor was given responsibility by President Johnson for issuing rules, regulations, and orders to carry out the nondiscrimination purposes of the Executive order and to determine compliance by contractors. Provision was made for the department to delegate its compliance enforcement powers to other federal administrative agencies for coverage of contractors in particular industries or sectors. Under such delegation, the Office for Civil Rights in the Department of

[2] Ibid. (p. 31). For good illustrations of such conflicting viewpoints, see Galbraith, Kuh, and Thurow (1971) and Bunzel (1973).

Health, Education, and Welfare administers the compliance reviews and applies the rules and regulations to colleges and universities, regardless of which federal agency awards the contract.[3] HEW's 10 regional offices have the responsibility, in the first instance, for determining whether a university is in compliance and for recommending possible enforcement action to the Department of Labor. In case of a finding of noncompliance with Executive Order No. 11246 as amended or with the rules, regulations, or orders issued by the Department of Labor, a university may have its federal research or other contracts canceled, terminated, or suspended in whole or in part, and the university may be declared ineligible for further federal contracts.

From December 1969 to January 1974, a total of 20 universities are recorded as having had a temporary block imposed on new contracts or renewals for failure either to supply the required data or to meet other compliance requirements, including the submission of an acceptable affirmative action plan.[4] The delayed contracts of those 20 institutions amounted to about $28.5 million. At least four other universities have been reported as experiencing some brief delay.

Complaints of discrimination may be of three kinds. *Pattern* complaints allege that a general pattern of discrimination exists at a college or university. A *class* complaint alleges that discrimination prevails against a particular class (or classes) of employees in an institution. An *individual* complaint involves a charge that the complainant has personally been subjected to discrimination in employment or in applying for employment; it can include a claim of discrimination against members of the complainant's class and, thus, include a class complaint.

Through its regional offices, the Office for Civil Rights has re-

[3] Except for colleges and universities, federal contract compliance is handled as part of the contracting process, with compliance reviews conducted by compliance officers on the staffs of the agencies that actually make the contracts with the contractors. Only in the case of institutions of higher education is all compliance supervision concentrated in a single agency (the Department of Health, Education, and Welfare), whatever the agencies with which universities conclude their research and other contracts.

[4] They were: Harvard, University of Michigan, Columbia, Cornell, Duke, Vanderbilt, Northwestern, Notre Dame, University of Illinois, Loyola University (New Orleans), Yeshiva, University of California at Berkeley and at San Diego, New Mexico State University, University of Arkansas, University of Texas, Rice University, Mt. Sinai School of Medicine, Virginia Polytechnic Institute, and University of Washington.

sponsibility for investigating pattern and class complaints against universities, and had such responsibility for the individual complaints of professional employees of universities until March 1972. Educational institutions were excluded from Title VII of the Civil Rights Act of 1964 until that exclusion was removed by enactment of the Equal Employment Opportunity Act in March 1972. Thereafter all individual complaints were to be handled by the Equal Employment Opportunity (EEO) Commission and not by HEW, which did, however, continue to handle some filed before March 1972.

Most of the complaints brought against colleges and universities have been on grounds of sex discrimination. In the spring of 1970, Harvard University was the first private institution and the University of Michigan the first public institution to be investigated by HEW as a result of complaints lodged against them. By mid-1973, pattern complaints on grounds of sex discrimination were reported to have been made against some 500 of the 2,500 institutions of higher education. Included in the 500 were practically all the major universities. Many of those complaints were brought by such women's advocacy organizations as the National Organization for Women and the Women's Equity Action League. A figure for the number of class complaints was not available at the time. By mid-1973, about 350 women had filed individual complaints against their institutions. Such actions have tended to put university administrators under considerable internal as well as external pressure.

In addition to enforcement of antibias requirements under federal contracts, HEW has enforcement powers under the Higher Education Amendments of 1972, which prohibit discrimination on the basis of sex in all federally assisted programs or activities.

The Higher Education Amendments of 1972 also extended to executive, administrative, and professional employees in colleges and universities the provisions of the Equal Pay Act of 1963. The Wage-Hour Division of the Department of Labor is the compliance agency for enforcing equal pay for women and men on jobs requiring equal skill, effort, and responsibility.

The Equal Employment Opportunity Act of 1972 amended Title VII (which deals with employment) of the Civil Rights Act of 1964 to include thereunder all educational institutions, whether they have federal assistance or not, and gave new enforcement powers to the Equal Employment Opportunity Commission. The commission (or the Attorney General in the case of public institutions) may bring a civil action in the federal courts against an institution, charging an unlawful employment practice, which may include a pattern of discrimination as well as an individual complaint.

Furthermore, about four-fifths of the states have fair employment practices laws, which usually ban discrimination in employment on grounds of race, sex, religion, or age. The laws in many states apply to the faculties of institutions of higher education and are generally administered by a state agency specifically created for that purpose. As provided in the Civil Rights Act of 1964, the federal commission defers action on charges until a state agency granted deferred status has acted on the same complaint.

Thus a university can be subject to as many as four separate compliance investigations over a period of time and can have separate charges of discrimination brought against it by three federal agencies and a state agency. The agencies have different data requirements and may apply somewhat different definitions, criteria, and standards for determining the existence and extent of discrimination. Indeed, as indicated in Chapter 7, enforcement may vary significantly among the 10 regional offices of HEW. Although coordination among the different federal and state enforcement agencies has improved somewhat, universities have been troubled by inconsistency and confusion in the enforcement of antidiscrimination laws and regulations. Also, universities that submitted affirmative action plans have often waited a year, two years, and even longer without definite and official word from HEW on whether their plans were acceptable as submitted. From November 1971 until July 23, 1973, some 33 affirmative action plans submitted by colleges and universities were given interim or final approval, 51 plans were rejected as not approvable under the Executive order and HEW's rules and regulations, and 175 were pending.[5] Those figures accounted for only about two-sevenths of the universities and colleges estimated to be under HEW regulation.

In addition to actions by government agencies, educational institutions can be sued directly in the federal and state courts by persons alleging that they have suffered discrimination. Universities have been confronted with an increasing number of such court suits under Title VII of the Civil Rights Act and state legislation. At the same time, a considerable number of charges of "reverse dis-

[5] Data obtained from letter sent by Gwendolyn Gregory of the Office for Civil Rights of HEW to Sheldon E. Steinbach of the American Council on Education, dated Sept. 17, 1973.

crimination" (favoring women and members of minorities) have been filed with HEW against academic institutions, and some have been taken directly to the courts.

CHARACTERISTICS OF MAJOR UNIVERSITIES

Universities are known for the quality of their faculties as educators and as creators of new knowledge through research, and for the relative effectiveness of their programs of undergraduate instruction and graduate training in the arts and sciences. It is mainly on their contributions in the humanities, social sciences, and physical sciences that the national and world reputation of American universities rests.

In addition to the education of students and the creation of new knowledge, universities serve as independent centers for the advanced study of human affairs and the critical evaluation of society. To perform those functions properly, academic freedom—freedom to search out and report the truth—is essential.

Compared with universities in other countries, American institutions of higher education have enjoyed an unusually large measure of autonomy and independence from government control.[6] That has been true not only of our private universities but also of the great state universities. Indeed, the state universities that have achieved the most distinction have generally enjoyed the greatest degree of autonomy.

In this book, special attention is given to the possible effects of government antidiscrimination regulation upon the faculties and the instruction-research programs of what are termed *major universities.* They are the three to four dozen most outstanding universities in the country in terms of advanced education and research in the arts and sciences.[7] Among the major universities in this country are such distinguished centers of learning as the University of California at Berkeley, Massachusetts Institute of Technology, and the universities of Chicago, Columbia, Harvard,

[6] For a comparative analysis of American universities and those in other countries, see Ben-David (1972).

[7] As used in this book, the term means those universities that rank in the top level according to such criteria as (1) assessments of the quality of programs of graduate education published by the American Council on Education and number of Ph.D. degrees granted per year and (2) measures of research contribution such as volume of scholarly publications, dollar volume of research, and honors received by faculty (e.g., Nobel Prize winners, members of the National Academy of Sciences, and awards by professional associations in academic disciplines).

Michigan at Ann Arbor, Princeton, Stanford, Wisconsin at Madison, and Yale.

Such institutions have not only been leaders in advanced instruction and scholarship but also tend to be selected by HEW as leaders in the development of detailed affirmative action plans that conform to federal regulations. In other words, they have been used to establish patterns, to provide early examples of approvable affirmative action plans.

Furthermore, the problems and issues of government regulation via affirmative action plans with numerical hiring goals tend to arise most acutely in cases involving the major universities. Many years of on-the-job training are required before one becomes a mature teacher-scholar who enjoys the combined advantages of academic tenure and academic freedom at such institutions.

A high degree of faculty self-governance generally characterizes major universities. The faculty determine the curriculum and largely control academic personnel decisions on such matters as recruitment, appointment, reappointment, promotion, and individual faculty salaries.

Our major universities generate a large proportion of the new knowledge and basic-research contributions in this country. Probably in no other country is national scientific endeavor so concentrated in universities as it is in the United States (see Kerr, 1972). A good part of our well-being rests on the effectiveness of their faculties.

While they share the goal of improving knowledge and training minds, the major universities differ in their traditions, in their administrative structures and practices, in the areas of their strength within different disciplines, and in their student-faculty relationships. And they are in strong competition with one another for financial and other community support, for the best undergraduate students, for the best graduate students in particular disciplines, and for the best faculty in different subject areas.

In American universities, the academic department is an important unit in the organization and governance of a university faculty, especially for purposes of the teaching and research programs and personnel decisions. Departments are generally organized according to academic disciplines. Within a department, tenured professors in their teaching and research tend to operate much like individual entrepreneurs, but they do, of course, have a strong self-interest in the successful operation and long-term future of that department. The aim is a kind of collegial form of self-government, motivated by a common desire for excellence. Excellence can be defined in terms of the institution's reputation for undergraduate instruction, for graduate training, and for research output, both inside the university and among teacher-scholars in the discipline around the country and in the world at large.

In a very real sense, the faculty are the university. The reputation and success of a university depends largely on the teaching and research ability, the dedication, and the collegial cooperation of the professoriate. Therefore, the trustees and the administration generally allow a considerable measure of autonomy to the faculty in teaching and research activities, and successful university administration involves working in cooperation with faculty in the definition and achievement of the educational objectives of the institution.

Although our analysis will focus on major institutions, much of it applies to other universities and distinguished colleges as well. A number of the less-prominent universities have at least one distinguished academic department and to that extent are part of the interuniversity competition for top-quality faculty. Also, major universities not infrequently compete for individual faculty with departments in such distinguished colleges as Amherst, Oberlin, Swarthmore, and Williams. In considering the problems of applying affirmative action guidelines, one needs to recognize that a fairly mixed situation exists in terms of the academic reputations of individual faculty in the 2,500 institutions of higher education in this country, of which some 900 come under federal contract compliance.

PLAN OF THE BOOK

This study of antibias regulation of major universities begins in Chapter 2 with an examination of faculty appointments at such institutions. An understanding of the universities' demand for faculty is basic for the analysis in the chapters that follow. A reader knowledgeable of university aims in hiring, promotion, and compensation of faculty may wish to skim or omit this chapter.

Chapter 3 considers the various aspects of discrimination, especially in university faculties, and explains the need to take supply factors into account in dealing with allegations of discrimination in employment. The federal government, in its method of analysis and its enforcement programs, has tended to neglect these factors. The supply analysis in this chapter provides a basis for much of the discussion in the next two chapters.

Chapters 4 and 5 critically examine the federal program of compliance for contractors, based on Executive orders and administrative decisions. This HEW program of compliance uses estimated proportional representation by sex and race to establish the extent of discrimination, and requires that the contractor adopt numerical hiring goals by sex and race in order to achieve that proportional representation. Chapter 4 is concerned especially with the development of the enforcement program of HEW and the prescribed scheme for estimating the statistical base for hiring goals to enforce proportional representation. Chapter 5 contains a critical analysis of numerical hiring goals calculated in the required manner and considers other goals for affirmative action plans.

The enforcement programs of other federal agencies and of state agencies, based on legislation, are considered in Chapter 6. They involve the investigation and prosecution of complaints filed with an agency or the courts by individuals alleging that they have been discriminated against on grounds of sex, race, or religion. Use of adversary proceedings to determine the comparative professional qualifications of individual faculty for appointment and promotion is examined, and a voluntary system for outside mediation and arbitration of individual complaints of discrimination in faculty employment is proposed.

Chapter 7 discusses the staff of the Higher Education Division of HEW and the requirements it enforces with respect to the affirmative action plans of universities and colleges. On the basis of experience, a single HEW regulatory unit for the major universities is recommended.

The faculty system of collegial decision making by a community of scholars and its long-term educational benefits are discussed in Chapter 8. The faculty system is contrasted with industry's hierarchical system of authority from the top down. The chapter explains the unsuitability of the industrial model for faculty decision making under government antibias regulation.

Chapter 9 presents an alternative program of antibias regulation for faculty of institutions of higher education. The program provides for systematic collection of faculty data from covered institutions and central analysis of the material for purposes of comparing the progress of the institutions and estimating the effects of the government's antibias programs as well as for enforcement purposes. The six substantive components of the program are based on the material and conclusions presented in preceding chapters.

The final chapter summarizes the principal faults in federal antibias regulation of universities, indicating that the seven main defects of federal regulatory programs can have as adverse consequences for most of the country's universities and colleges subject to regulation as they have for major universities. The chapter discusses the need for leadership by faculty and administrators to achieve appropriate and constructive antibias programs on the part of both the universities and the government.

2. The Operation of Faculty Appointment Systems

Antibias programs and government regulation for antibias purposes need to take proper account of the systems for faculty appointment and promotion in leading universities. Those systems have evolved over a long span of time and are peculiar to higher education in countries of the Western world. They involve special procedures for faculty evaluation and selection of candidates, and they play a crucial role in determining faculty quality and the achievement by universities of their educational goals.

Unfortunately, university administrators and faculty are finding that things they assume are well known about the functioning of their systems for faculty appointment and advancement are often not understood and appreciated, and are passed off lightly by federal officials and others who press distinguished universities to make commitments to increase sharply the number of women and blacks and members of other minorities in their faculties. Consciously or unconsciously, efforts are being made, in the name of antidiscrimination, to transform those faculty systems—to make them conform more closely to industrial patterns of personnel management.

Such developments present a challenge to the faculties and top administrations of major universities, to whom the country looks for leadership in higher education. The public needs to be informed of the significance of those faculty systems for the successful accomplishment of the educational programs of universities, and the universities need to reexamine their systems of faculty appointment and advancement to make sure that they are as free of bias—race, sex, and other forms—as is humanly possible. That message runs throughout this book and is given special emphasis in the last chapter.

This chapter discusses the planning, the appointment procedures, the demand competition, and the drive for faculty excellence that characterize major universities. It explains the costliness of tenure appointments that prove unsatisfactory—"mistakes"—and the need to take account of faculty development in formulating and enforcing government programs for preventing bias in faculty recruitment, appointment, and advancement.

PLANNING FOR EXCELLENCE

Major universities generally strive, especially in the selection of tenured faculty, to achieve teaching and scholarship of the highest order. The tenured faculty play the central role in determining the intellectual quality of the institution and in shaping its long-term character and reputation.

To develop and retain a distinguished and effective faculty in the face of severe competition among the three or four dozen major universities requires a great deal of thoughtful planning, skillful recruitment, and careful development of an environment that fosters productive academic careers. Great academic departments and outstanding faculties do not come about by the mechanistic application of procedures or by a willingness to settle for the very good instead of the very best. They are usually the result of intelligent efforts and leadership on the part of many faculty and members of the administration.

In planning for the most effective use of the resources available for faculty staffing of a department or all departments in the arts and sciences in a university, the faculty and the administration need to think in terms of the educational objectives of the institution. In what kind of a program of teaching and research should the university excel? How much stress should there be on undergraduate teaching, on graduate teaching, on sponsored research projects? How wide a coverage of disciplines should a particular university try to achieve? In what subfields of the different disciplines should it seek to have great strength? What methods of instruction, and in what proportions, seem best suited for its educational program? What research best fits its faculty and physical facilities?

Especially in major universities, research and teaching reinforce each other. The search for new knowledge helps teaching to continue to be fresh and stimulating throughout a professor's tenure, and the critical interchange between advanced student and creative scholar sharpens and improves the research product. Students are thus able to gain insights into the exacting and imaginative work involved in creating new knowledge by scholarly and scientific methods and disciplined diligence.

Planning for a department, a group of departments, and the whole faculty involves not only drawing proper balances among undergraduate teaching, graduate teaching, and particular kinds of research, but also thinking about the needs for the next academic year within a long-range framework. Assistant professors are usually hired for a three- to five-year term; promotions to tenure, which normally extends to retirement, usually involve an employment commitment averaging between 30 and 35 years.

In addition to the foregoing, planning for excellence of a departmental faculty has to take account of such other factors as the following:

The specific amounts of teaching time by subfield required to staff needed courses, semester by semester, taking account of scheduled leaves of absence

Awareness of the dynamics of the discipline in order to anticipate student requirements and to take advantage of developing prospects for particular research enterprises

Arrangement for sufficient versatility in the teaching staff to furnish the flexibility needed to meet short-term changes and long-range trends in the discipline

Provision of sufficient diversity among the faculty to meet student and research needs—such as differences in approach and methods of analysis, differences in background and views in subjects where values and policy issues are important factors in instruction, and differences in sex, race, and cultural experience to provide breadth of understanding and role models, which may be especially important for undergraduate instruction

Retention of sufficient nontenure positions and turnover among junior faculty to supply the stimulus and invigorating influence of able, fresh recruits to the discipline, who are trained under other masters of their subject, and to provide opportunity for the department to select for promotion to tenure on the basis of a period of experience as a junior faculty member at the institution

Continuation and enhancement of an institution's reputation in certain subfields and disciplines gained as a result of the research contributions and training in the profession provided by previous faculty—in other words, the retention of traditional strengths and historical advantages of the department and the university

Faculty diversity is a complex subject that involves a variety of aspects and considerations. Faculty members differ with regard to: (1) their abilities for particular types of teaching, (2) their approaches and methods of scholarship, (3) their sheer intellectual ability and dedication to scholarship, (4) their gifts for intellectual leadership and administration, (5) their philosophies of life and education, (6) their cultural background and range of experience, (7) their political-social viewpoints and activism for reform, (8) their race, sex, and national origin, and (9) many other aspects. Individual faculty members have different combinations of these characteristics and generally are quite individualistic.

Particular kinds of diversity serve particular educational and intellectually creative purposes. Natives of an area can enrich area studies. Diversity of intellectual approach and philosophy may be more creative and educationally significant in the humanities and social sciences than in the physical sciences and engineering. Diversity of race, religion, and sex may be more important for student-faculty relationships and student role-models at the undergraduate level than at the graduate level, and it may be of greater significance in some settings and times than in other circumstances and periods.

In considering the question of appropriate diversity for a faculty, one should think in terms of balance among objectives and the area of focus for such balance. Proper diversity can improve breadth of understanding and provide challenge to conventional wisdom and unthinking conformity. But challenge just for challenge's sake can promote dilettantism and be nonconstructive. There is a question on the need for, and kind of, diversity in particular academic departments and on whether diversity should be considered and judged in terms of its distribution by department, by divisions of the arts and sciences departments, or over the arts and sciences faculty as a whole. A single pattern of diversity applied to each and every discipline in a uniform fashion would be a kind of uniformity—a contradiction of diversity. It would tend to injure the very values that diversity should promote.[1]

Faculty diversity, to be constructive, must involve tolerance and

[1] Advocacy groups are prone to overlook the many dimensions and the differentiation inherent in the concept of academic diversity in their single-minded pursuit of one goal. The Office for Civil Rights in the Department of Health, Education, and Welfare in compliance enforcement at institutions of higher learning has also been subject to the same criticism. This matter is discussed further in Chapter 5.

respect for appropriate differences among colleagues. Effective functioning of academic departments requires a readiness on the part of independent operators enjoying academic freedom to cooperate in the achievement of common departmental and university objectives, to pursue the truth in a collegial atmosphere of friendly rivalry. Above all, one should bear in mind the importance, especially for major universities, of the intellectual quality of the faculty and its combined ability to achieve the educational objectives of the institution.

ATTRACTING OUTSTANDING TEACHER-SCHOLARS

Major universities in this country compete for leading scientists, social scientists, and humanities scholars throughout the universe of advanced learning. In considering the recruitment and development of outstanding faculty, one needs to distinguish between mature teacher-scholars who are considered for a tenure position and "fresh" Ph.D.'s who are considered for term appointments. The latter are regarded as probationary employees gaining further training and experience in order to qualify for a tenure appointment at some institution.

Leading scholars usually have to be attracted away from tenure professorships that are satisfactory to them. These scholars generally have experienced numerous attempts to woo them to other universities. Their decisions to stay or to move are likely to hinge on the comparative advantages of positions at the competing universities—on which place they think would best facilitate their research contributions and would afford them the best opportunity to teach and develop outstanding young scholars.

Some of the leading teacher-scholars are so generally able and contribute so much to the work of their colleagues and the university enterprise that any major university would consider it a great achievement to attract one of them to its faculty. Other prominent scholars and scientists may not be effective in certain types of teaching and may be oriented almost exclusively toward their own research and research staff. Their scholarly reputations may make them academic ornaments, but some universities may decide that scholars of such limited usefulness are too costly in terms of meeting institutional needs and the disturbing repercussions that their appointment at a very high salary and with very special advantages would have on the tenured faculty in the department and in the university in general. Departments at universities that do not have "research professorships," and have a single faculty teaching in both the undergraduate and graduate programs, would not seek to attract such a "limited" contributor to their university's educational goals unless (1) the department was anxious for added prominence in research or (2) it was well staffed with faculty who had the attributes that the "star" lacked, and his or her subfield was one in which the university wished to be eminent in scholarly terms.

The most distinguished teacher-scholars are normally not in the market looking for jobs as is the case with students who are just completing their Ph.D. training or is the case with many junior faculty who, in their early probation years, are searching for career identity and often move between institutions as a part of that process. And a major university with a senior position does not normally need to canvass the market to discover or observe the supply being offered. The tenured members of a department as a group are likely to know who the top teacher-scholars are in the subfield where there is an opening. If one is thinking in such terms as reputation in the discipline and drawing power for the most able graduate students, the best-qualified teacher-scholars for a tenure opening should be well recognized by scholars in the discipline. That is especially true in the physical sciences, where a strong relationship appears to exist between the significance or quality of a scientist's contributions (as measured by citations of his or her published work) and both awards received and appointment in high-ranking departments.[2]

To avoid a charge of sex or racial bias, universities nowadays generally follow a procedure that involves some public announcement of both tenure and nontenure openings. Whether or not past experience has proved such announcement of value in recruitment for senior faculty positions, because of HEW pressure in affirmative action plans and in compliance reviews, money and time are spent for that purpose.[3]

[2] See Cole and Cole (1967). Also, analysis shows that the system of using scientists as "referees" with respect to selection or rejection of papers submitted for publication to a leading scientific journal can serve to avoid any special bias of selection in terms of the authors' ages, scientific reputations, academic positions, etc. See Merton and Zuckerman (1973).

[3] Universities in Great Britain and the Scandinavian countries have for decades advertised open professorships as a standard practice. However, the ratio of female faculty to male faculty in Britain and the three Scandinavian countries seems, on the whole, to be lower than in this country. See Galenson (1973, pp. 27, 29).

When a decision has been made on the best-suited teacher-scholar for a tenure position, every effort is made to attract him or her to the university. If it cannot attract its first choice, a major university may leave a tenure post open, filling the vacancy temporarily with visitors or junior faculty until the university can obtain the very best mature scholar. It may give a standing offer to the professor considered the best person for an open professorship, or may wait two or three years and make a second offer to the top-ranked scholar who declined to move on the first offer. In a surprising number of cases, the second offer is accepted. Standing offers may also be made to a leading teacher-scholar without regard to an institution's need in a particular subfield. That might be done because of that professor's breadth of scholarly interests and the contributions that a powerful mind can make to the intellectual life of a university community.

A university trying to attract a distinguished professor will seek to make its offer as close to his or her desires as possible, without violating its teaching norms and appropriate salary relationships. Discussions concerning various aspects of the university and the offer—benefit comparisons, collegial relationships, housing, the relative advantages of living in the community, etc.—will be held with the professor and his or her family. A mature professor is likely to weigh all aspects because a move may be costly in terms of interruption of work and of adjustments to new conditions and because any move could be the last one. And, of course, the professor's present university will undoubtedly make a counteroffer.

The process of recruitment and appointment is typically much more market-like in hiring persons who have recently earned a Ph.D. degree or are close to it (normally the Ph.D. is a prerequisite for entering on the promotional ladder at a university). The new Ph.D. supply available each year is about one-seventh the size of the nation's faculty members who hold Ph.D. degrees. Of course, many Ph.D.'s in engineering and science go into nonacademic employment. Universities usually hire junior faculty (assistant professors and instructors) in much larger numbers than senior faculty (associate and full professors). For instance, junior hires recently have been running at a rate 5 to 10 times the figure for senior hires at some major universities.

Enforcement of equal employment opportunity for women and minority persons is vital when they are ready for their first regular teaching position. That is true because: (1) there is a possibility that some new Ph.D.'s of great promise will not be known by leading scholars in a subfield;[4] (2) with considerable uncertainty of the ultimate performance of individuals and the limited commitment of a nontenure appointment, universities may be justified in making some high-talent but high-risk appointments where the probability that the appointee will achieve great distinction may be as low as one out of four; (3) experience in the early years is very important in determining the career level that one aspires to reach; and (4) it is most desirable that those who have the capability to reach the top in the academic profession have the proper environment and opportunities (including free time for research) to permit the full development of their talents and contributions.

It is at the stage of first full-time appointment to a position on the ladder of promotion that any "pattern of discrimination" in faculty employment can best be established by objective analysis. Major universities seek to appoint persons to assistant professorships from among the most promising as teachers and scholars in the current crop of Ph.D.'s[5]

Even during the current period of oversupply of Ph.D.'s relative to demand, especially for positions at the major universities, there is strong competition among leading departments for Ph.D.'s they believe have the greatest promise. Ph.D.'s assumed to be the most promising candidates are likely to receive offers from several major universities at about the same time of the year—December, January, and February.

Factors that can influence the decision of a strong candidate include the following: the salary and rank offered; the prospects for a tenure opening later on in the candidate's specialty; teaching loads; free time for research, including paid leave for that purpose; research support and facilities; other benefits, including pensions; the quality and congeniality of the faculty in the department; the quality of the students; the university's financial condition; and the kind of leadership the university's administration provides.

Excellence attracts excellence. To draw new faculty of the highest quality to junior positions, a university should have a first-class

[4] Ph.D. candidates of high quality often earn reputations as graduate students while working on their theses by such means as the submission and publication of articles at that stage and the presentation of papers or participation in discussions at annual meetings of the professional association in the discipline.

[5] The sex ratio for the top group of new Ph.D.'s in a discipline might differ from the sex ratio for all new Ph.D.'s in that discipline. However, one can probably assume that the average quality of all female new Ph.D.'s and all male new Ph.D.'s in any one year is approximately equal.

academic reputation. Able and ambitious new Ph.D.'s may wish to spend their early years in the profession at a leading university for the "career development" benefits that professional experience there can provide. And, even though it offers little prospect for a tenure opening in a certain subfield, a leading university may be a very favorable place from which to obtain an attractive post elsewhere.

THE FACULTY'S ROLE IN ACHIEVING EXCELLENCE

As already explained, the faculty in leading universities usually enjoys a large measure of self-governance. Indeed, there seems to be a fairly close correlation between an institution's standing in the scholarly world and the control that the faculty enjoys over its own affairs. At the highest levels of academe, the faculty, through the department structure and a facultywide appointments committee, practically exercises the power to select new faculty, to judge which faculty members should not be reappointed and which should be promoted to tenure, and, in many institutions, to decide faculty salaries and salary increases for individual faculty. Essentially, the tenured faculty are the employers of faculty in leading institutions, and any charges of discrimination in faculty employment are, for the most part, really made against faculty members in the performance of their faculty responsibilities.

Leaders among the faculties of major universities place great store on significant contributions to knowledge through the disciplined methods of scholarship and science. For outstanding contributions, teacher-scholars are singled out for rewards of various kinds—rapid promotion, professional awards and honors, ample research support, and other forms of academic distinction and privilege. At the top reaches of academia, there is a considerable amount of "discrimination by distinction."

In a leading university, the tenured faculty of a department should have the primary responsibility for recommending new appointments, reappointments, and promotions and also for judging the salaries that assistant and associate professors merit. Most of the tenured members of a high-ranking department should know by reputation the leading teacher-scholars in the discipline, should be in a good position to judge the qualifications most needed in a candidate for an open position in the department,[6] and generally should have a strong professional interest in hiring an outstanding

[6] For joint appointments in two departments or where interdepartmental programs are involved in appointments, a proposed appointment would be critically examined by the two or more departments or organizational units.

performer and an effective colleague. Tenured faculty tend to have a fairly long perspective on the department and have an extensive experience with the development of graduate students, junior faculty, and senior faculty on which to base their judgment of a candidate's promise as a teacher-scholar in that setting.

From the viewpoint of long-run benefit to the institution, perhaps the most important function that the tenured professors of a department perform is to select and attract the best persons for tenure appointments. Usually a great deal of time, effort, and care are devoted to that process.

Rather typically, the department selects from its members a search committee to study the scholarly work, the teaching qualities, and the potential contributions to the department and the university of mature teacher-scholars in the subfield who appear to be among the best suited for the post. The search committee obtains all the significant information it can on the leading candidates and makes a report to the tenured members of the department, possibly ranking the leading candidates and recommending one as the best. The department goes over the material, with other members reading the writings and possibly collecting additional confidential material from personal sources. When the department's tenured faculty are satisfied that the canvass of the subfield, the available material on candidates, and the analysis of their strengths and weaknesses are complete and according to requirements, they vote on a recommendation that an offer be made to the candidate considered best qualified for the post.[7]

The department's recommendation is then sent to the administration, where it is checked for conformance to procedures and completeness of documentation. The procedure in many major institutions provides for solicitation by (say) the dean of the faculty of letters from distinguished outside scholars in the field and subfield, asking, on a strictly confidential basis, for an evaluation of the recommended candidate as a teacher-scholar and for a comparison of his or her qualifications with other professors of recognized excellence in that subfield in this country and abroad. When the confidential outside letters and any other additional material are available, the procedure may require that the depart-

[7] The department's tenured faculty could decide at this point that no possible candidate is sufficiently distinguished and promising as a teacher-scholar in the future for appointment to a professorship and instead have the opening converted to a nontenure or a visiting appointment for the time being.

ment's recommendation be presented to a higher-level committee, perhaps a standing faculty committee on appointments (technically advisory to the president and elected by the faculty) for its review.[8]

Review by an overall faculty or faculty-administration committee on appointments has certain advantages. Such a committee is able to judge a department's appointment recommendation on a broader, less parochial basis; it is in a position to compare the quality of recommendations coming from the different departments; and it has additional material on which to base a judgment. That additional material includes the outside confidential letters of evaluation, which, generally speaking, are remarkably frank and informative and often contain quite thoughtful analysis of the subfield and comparative assessments of individuals as teacher-scholars.

The committee on appointments makes its recommendations, both for and against, to the president—who usually accepts them, presenting the favorable ones to the trustees for final approval. Experience indicates that faculty-appointments committees are apt to reject more department recommendations for promotion to tenure of faculty from within than recommendations for appointments to tenure from outside. Partly, that is because a number of contemplated appointments from outside may be headed off by the deans and the president's raising questions with the department chairman before a formal recommendation is made by the tenured members of the department.

Faculty assessment of an assistant professor for promotion to tenure based on a five- to seven-year period of experience, which ends in a decision either to promote or to terminate, is a very severe form of testing. During that period, assistant professors at major institutions are under great pressure to achieve an outstanding record in scholarship, in teaching, and in other contributions to the university that compares favorably with the record of scholars in their field at other universities. Such a record generally requires intense dedication to the task of achieving a national and inter-

[8] The procedure outlined is very similar to that in effect at Princeton, Stanford, and a number of other universities. Under the Harvard system, the department reports and recommendation for a tenure appointment are submitted to an "ad hoc committee," composed of several inside faculty from different departments and several outside scholars. The committee meets with the president and the dean of the faculty. At Princeton the deans and the president meet with the committee in a series of meetings that review departmental recommendations concerning reappointments, promotions, new outside appointments in the tenure ranks, and salary increases in the three professional ranks.

national reputation in one's field for scholarly accomplishment and promise of further accomplishment. In some cases, promotion cannot be achieved because no appropriate tenure opening exists in the assistant professor's subfield at that university.

At most major universities, probably less than half of those who are appointed assistant professors are promoted to continuing tenure. At Princeton University, for example, in the early 1960s about one out of three who were appointed assistant professors eventually achieved tenure; by the late 1960s and early 1970s, that ratio had declined to about one out of four, despite an apparent increase in the average quality of assistant professors.[9] In the arts and sciences at Harvard University, the ratio is considerably lower; assistant professorships there are, for the most part, considered as temporary appointments for one five-year term.

With such severe competition for tenure appointments and so much of the university's future riding on them, it is important to make certain that the universities have proper procedures to assure open and equal opportunity in recruitment and that they base assessment of qualifications on as much valid information and expert judgment as possible. In the enforcement of nondiscrimination in university faculty hiring and advancement, the Office for Civil Rights of the U.S. Department of Health, Education, and Welfare should place more stress and store on proper procedures properly applied and less on questionable statistical estimates.

The faculty procedures are less well-suited for handling appointments outside the regular ranks, such as a lecturer appointment. That is so because candidates for those positions generally are selected on grounds other than scholarly achievement or promise. Such special nonscholarly appointments include persons hired as native-speaking teachers of such foreign languages as Arabic, Chinese, Japanese, Russian, and Turkish. They also include skilled artists in the visual arts: dancers, painters, film makers, and sculptors. Distinguished scholars may find it somewhat difficult to assess the university performance and academic promise of faculty performing such services. Persons in such special categories of faculty are often hired for undergraduate instruction and for short periods of time. The purpose and terms of their appointment need to be clearly defined and mutually understood if they are not to feel discriminated against in cases where their appointments con-

[9] For a discussion of the factors and procedures in promotion to tenure at Princeton, see *An Information Statement for the Guidance of New Faculty at Princeton University* (1972).

tinue over a considerable period of time and then are terminated or do not lead to promotion.

THE COSTLINESS OF MISTAKES

At leading institutions, an outside appointment to a professorship carries tenure upon appointment, and an outside appointment to an associate professorship either does, or practically does, carry tenure.[10] Appointments that turn out to be mistakes can be quite costly unless the disappointing faculty member can be induced to leave. Since he or she has been a disappointment as a teacher-scholar in a major university, rival universities may not have an interest in hiring that faculty member away.

A teacher-scholar may, over time, develop serious shortcomings. For example, he or she may have a block on publication of his or her theoretical work or research results. If the faculty member has a lively, innovative mind and makes contributions through the effects his or her ideas have on the published work of students and colleagues, that may not be a serious drawback. However, a department in a major university can afford only a limited number of oral-tradition, publication-shy scholars.

Other types of mistakes are more serious. The faculty member on tenure appointment may lack the mental capacity or the drive to do the hard work of advanced teaching and research necessary to become a major figure in his or her field. The scholarly efforts of such a faculty member may consist largely of tidying up the edges of a system of thought of a distinguished professor. Over time both the teaching and research contributions of the faculty member become less and less interesting or important. Similarly, in dynamic disciplines, the faculty member's professional training may be rendered obsolete by the development of new research methods and analytical techniques or of new branches of the discipline, thus reducing the effectiveness of his or her teaching and research activities.[11] Or, the attention and energies of the faculty

[10] Often an initial appointment of associate professor from outside is made as a three-year appointment which, if renewed, carries tenure. Normally, much the same procedure is followed for appointment to associate professor as for appointment to tenure, and the initial appointment is followed by a further appointment carrying tenure in practically all cases. Only a great disappointment with the person's performance would cause a refusal to reappoint an associate professor from outside.

[11] In biochemistry it is said that the field is developing so fast and the competition for scientific contributions is so keen that, over a five-year period, practically all knowledge becomes obsolete, and professors have to spend an extraordinary amount of time on their research and on preparation for teaching advanced courses.

member may be drained off into outside consulting or other off-campus activities that contribute little to the growth and intellectual enrichment of a teacher-scholar so that his or her academic contributions suffer. For some of these adverse developments in individual cases, a department's faculty or a department's chairman or the university administration, singly or in combination, may share some of the responsibility for the decline. They may have failed to encourage and advise the faculty member and to help him or her to adjust to changes. One reason for stressing research and paid leaves of absence for scholarship is the stimulus to renewal and growth that they provide.

Finally, the faculty member's failure to live up to expectations may be due to nervous breakdowns, alcoholism, severe family problems, or other personal handicaps. The strenuous competition at high levels in academic life and the severe judgment of faculty by able students (reflected in their selection and evaluation of courses and choice of dissertation supervisors) may cause a sensitive faculty member to feel great strain.

As a faculty member's comparative effectiveness as a teacher and scholar declines, his or her usefulness to the department and university becomes more and more limited. He or she is not used so much for graduate teaching, is not invited to give papers or seminars on research achievements, and is less able to raise adequate funding for research. Colleagues in the department, including junior faculty, have less respect for his or her judgment; nevertheless, the professor, though declining in professional status, continues as a tenured member of the department to vote on new appointments, reappointments, and promotions. The relatively ineffective professor may be blocking the subfield either for appointment of a much more able teacher-scholar from outside or for promotion of an outstanding assistant professor in the department to tenure in that subfield.

Over time, the unsatisfactory professor's situation becomes increasingly embarrassing and difficult. Under a merit system of pay based on performance, the professor may receive either no salary increase or a very small one each year, as a result of evaluation of his contributions by the chairman of the department, the faculty appointments or review committee, and the deans. His or her discontent may have unfortunate effects on the department's faculty meetings. Complaints may be made to the administration. Eventually, the professor may charge that he or she is being discriminated against unfairly in various ways—in salary, promotion, the granting of paid leaves for scholarship, the allocation of department and university research funds, the warnings colleagues give to students about the professor's courses, etc. If the professor can do so, he or she may decide to file a complaint with a federal or state civil rights compliance agency, alleging discrimination on grounds of sex, race, or religion.

With a well-developed appointments' procedure and professional handling of cases by the departmental faculty and the administration under that procedure, the uncorrectible "mistakes" at any one time can be confined to no more than 2 percent of the tenured faculty. Weaknesses in procedure or stress on nonprofessional standards is likely to lead to a much higher percentage.[12]

It is, of course, especially troublesome if the "mistakes" tend to be concentrated in one department or a few departments. Where that is the case, it may be difficult to improve faculty quality because such departments would not be attractive to outstanding teacher-scholars or students. Also, in enforcing antidiscrimination laws and regulations, compliance officials may argue that female and minority-group assistant professors are fully qualified for an opening if their training, teaching, and scholarship are equal to the qualifications of some tenured professors in that department.[13] Given a universitywide ratio of, say, only one out of four assistant

[12] This is not the place to argue the pros and cons of academic tenure. The author believes that for major universities the tenure system has been, on balance, beneficial in terms of the quality and the performance of the faculty. In promotion cases, tenure provides junior faculty with a definite goal and forces the department's tenured faculty to make a final, well-documented decision on an assistant professor by a specific date, following an adequate period of experience. Tenure encourages professors to take a long-range view of the university's needs and their own careers, including research plans. It makes them more willing to take on tasks (such as department chairmanships and committee assignments) for the good of the university apart from their teaching and research. The security that tenure provides facilitates a collegial atmosphere and, under academic freedom of inquiry, candid criticism of university affairs and colleagues' work; the small number of "mistakes" in granting tenure and the possible disincentive of security to high productivity in an unfavorable environment normally are not sufficient to offset such advantages. For an article pointing to the advantages of tenure in distinguished universities, see Brewster (1972). See also *Discussion Memorandum on Academic Tenure at Harvard University* (1971); the system of Ad Hoc Committees on Permanent Appointments is explained pp. 36–40. For a recent comprehensive analysis of faculty tenure see Commission on Academic Tenure (1973).

[13] Revised Order No. 4 (Title 41 of the Code of Federal Regulations, Chapter 60-2.24 f5) states: "Neither minority nor female employees should be required to possess higher qualifications than those of the lowest qualified incumbent." See also Weitzman (1973, p. 484).

professors able to continue on through to promotion to tenure, pressures are likely to be very strong indeed to have women and blacks among those promoted in order to meet numerical goals and to have more racial and sexual "diversity" in the faculty. Such pressures, if effective, are likely to increase the percentage of "mistakes," especially in relatively weak departments. Unfortunately, "mistakes" in many instances do not become very evident for 5, 10, or even 15 years, but the tenure period amounts to 30 to 35 years.

SOME IMPLICATIONS FOR ANTIBIAS REGULATION

The facts set forth in this chapter need to be taken into account in federal and state programs of enforcement of nondiscrimination for the faculties of major universities.

The hiring of tenured faculty in leading institutions is a much more individualistic and carefully considered matter than is generally appreciated. It may make little sense, indeed it may be positively misleading in the case of major institutions, to think in terms of an ill-defined pool of supposedly qualified and available candidates from which judgments are made about the existence or nonexistence of discrimination and on the basis of which universities are to establish numerical goals for their hiring of women and blacks. And, as previously mentioned, it should be realized that charges of discrimination in faculty employment are likely to be directed at the faculty and to imply criticism of faculty procedures, which may, in some instances, need improvement.

There are significant differences among major universities and among academic departments within major universities. Leading institutions vary in size, traditions, governing structures and practices, and educational methods and goals. Vital to America's institutions of higher learning are their independence and the competition among them that is partly based on their differences. A government enforcement program should not, in the name of antidiscrimination, seek to impose a single pattern or set of procedures in a mechanistic, routine manner upon the internal operations and practices of all universities.

One of the great strengths of American universities is the drive their faculties have for improved quality and the opportunity that opens up for persons of diverse background to teach and write their way to the top in the world of science and scholarship. Makers and enforcers of antidiscrimination regulations should be careful not to impose requirements that blunt that professional drive and discourage salary differentials according to merit of performance as teacher-scholars.

Civil rights rule-makers and compliance enforcers need to recognize that graduate study leading to a Ph.D. degree is not the qualifying experience for a tenure position at a major university. The testing period is usually the first five to seven years after completing the requirements for a Ph.D. It is during those years that one demonstrates whether he or she has the intellectual capacity, the ingenuity and originality, the discipline and career dedication to make the outstanding contributions necessary to be a leading teacher-scholar in one's age group in a disciplinary subfield. The age range during which those qualities are demonstrated is usually between 25 and 35.[14]

When major institutions continue to promote to tenure only one out of three or one out of four highly selected assistant professors and the ratio turns out to be that unfavorable for female assistant professors, will the government enforcers recognize that that result is to be expected? Or will they press their aim "to increase materially the utilization of minorities and women at all levels where deficiencies exist"? And will some of the women not promoted (and thus terminated) and their supporters insist that the university is not properly carrying out its "affirmative action obligation"? And will those views lead not to the use of regular faculty self-government procedures for a hearing and ruling by a committee of faculty peers on cases of alleged unfair treatment in relation to appointment, reappointment, promotion, or academic rights but to the filing of a formal complaint with a government compliance agency or a court?

Those are the kinds of questions that press for attention as one studies recent experience and thinks about the future of our major universities in a period of increasing federal and state government intrusion into their governance.

[14] As is explained in the next chapter, that age range is likely to be a difficult one for women who seek to combine both a professional career aimed at the top and marriage and children.

3. *Discrimination and Qualified Supply*

Discrimination in employment pervades all advanced societies. An enterprise generally tries to select employees who will work well together under its kind of supervision and who have the potential for promotion to more responsible positions. Employer preference for "our type of employee" may be based on past experience, employee opinion, management's personal prejudices, unsupported assumptions, and any number of other influences. Firms, through in-plant training and in other ways, invest in developing an efficient work force; selection of the "right people" for particular jobs is a key element in that process.[1]

It is theoretically conceivable that employers' preferences could be distributed—locally, industrially, and occupationally—to reflect a true cross section of the total supply. In that case, all workers with the same qualifications could have equal employment opportunity. The supply itself would, of course, reflect any lack of equal opportunity that individuals might have experienced with respect to the particular kind and amount of preemployment training and experience required to acquire the necessary qualifications.

Actually, individual employer discrimination in hiring and employment presents a serious problem, especially for a democratic society, because it tends to be concentrated against certain classes and groups and to be more prevalent in some occupations than in others.

Theoretically, employer competition for workers should eliminate discrimination in employment and pay. Competitive forces should operate to have persons in a locality who have identical qualifications receive the same pay and have equal opportunity for employment in a job stressing those qualifications. Actually, market forces

[1] For a statement of views of managements concerning their preferences in hiring workers for manufacturing operations, see Lester (1954, pp. 53–68).

have not served to eliminate fully discrimination in pay or hiring; indeed, they seem, in many cases, not to have been very effective in significantly reducing the economic consequences of discrimination on the individuals directly affected, even over long periods of time.

Because the market has been relatively ineffective in solving many aspects of discrimination in employment against women and blacks and members of other minorities, government corrective action has been taken in the form of legislation, Executive orders, and regulations.

The term *discrimination* has been loosely used, often to ascribe blame and charge guilt without really knowing just what is meant. Strictly speaking, sex discrimination in employment would occur if men with exactly the same qualifications[2] as women were given preference in hiring, advancement, or pay; racial discrimination would occur if, in the same circumstances, a white person were given such preference over a black person. In each case, the reverse would also be true; if a woman or a black were given preference, there would be sex or racial discrimination. Where ability and other attributes are not identical, selection of a man with a better combination of qualifications for the job over a woman, or a white over a black, would not constitute sex or racial discrimination. Discrimination could occur at an earlier stage, however, in the form of unequal opportunity to obtain the necessary education and other qualifications for a particular position.

Education can play an important role in the elimination of prejudice and the development of personal talents, so that individuals enjoy more freedom to choose and enter appropriate careers and can advance in them according to their ability, ambition, hard work, and available job openings. Mainly, education helps to eliminate barriers to opportunity for individuals—whatever their skin color or sex—so that they can become part of the qualified supply for a profession or other high-level position requiring advanced university training.

As leaders in the world of higher learning in the humanities and the social and physical sciences, distinguished universities play a

[2] It would be most extraordinary for two candidates for a particular faculty position to have a combination of qualities for university teaching and for research contributions that is identical, or even "essentially equal." That is one reason that discrimination on grounds of sex, race, etc., may be difficult to prove in some cases.

major role in encouraging and developing highly talented supply, while, as a part of the demand, they employ some of that supply. Because they are so important on the supply and demand sides, the faculty of major universities are likely to be sensitive to university obligations in both aspects. As teachers, they are very much aware of both the beneficial consequences that the elimination of bias has for education and the social cost when talent is underdeveloped because it is blocked by discrimination.

In this chapter, supply for faculty positions in major institutions will be examined first for women and then for blacks. Many aspects of the discrimination problem, especially in universities, are different for women and blacks. That fact has too often been disregarded in antidiscrimination programs and legislation and by enforcement officials.

Basically, the qualifications for nontenure positions or for tenure positions in major universities should be the same regardless of race, sex, religion, or ethnic background. As suggested above, the qualifications for nontenured faculty can be described as follows: (1) intellectual ability and scholarly promise, demonstrated as a graduate student, that would rate one in the top group of the new Ph.D.'s in the discipline in the country;[3] (2) special competence in the subfield or combination of subfields, because openings in a discipline usually carry subfield qualifications even at the nontenure level; and (3) special abilities in teaching, research, and administrative matters that suit the institution's educational goals and student population and complement the teaching and research capabilities of the existing departmental staff.

For tenured faculty, as previously explained, qualified supply needs to be defined in even more individual and special terms, and the basis for judging qualifications is one's performance in teaching, scholarship, and colleagueship during the first five to seven years as an assistant professor.[4] Generally speaking, a national or inter-

[3] One might say top decile to indicate the kind of intellectual ability for academic work that major universities would expect to have for faculty appointment. However, as high as a quarter to half of the Ph.D.'s being turned out at a particular major university might be among those in the top decile for the whole country, in view of the selectivity it may be able to exercise in admissions and the high quality of its graduate program in that discipline.

[4] In disciplines and subfields such as advanced mathematics, theoretical physics, and economic theory, one may gain an international reputation for distinguished contributions that qualify the individual for a tenure position at a major institution in less than five years.

national reputation as an outstanding teacher-scholar is a necessary qualification. Beyond that, each institution seeks the person best suited for its particular needs over the projected period of a faculty member's tenureship.

DISCRIMINATION AGAINST WOMEN

Much of what is loosely called sex discrimination in employment is, at least partly, the consequence of choices made by women that are not attributable to a particular university. Those choices—of courses in secondary school and college, of occupation, and of marriage and children—may, of course, have been greatly influenced by notions concerning the proper role for women that are held by parents, friends, teachers, placement officers, and employers.

An example will indicate the problem of assessing responsibility or blame for the lack of female faculty in particular disciplines in universities. Women hold less than a half of 1 percent of the Ph.D. degrees in engineering and constitute a smaller percentage than that of the faculty members in engineering in universities. (By way of contrast, women in Russia represent perhaps 15 percent of those holding the degree that is equivalent to a Ph.D. in engineering and have been about 11 percent of the engineering teaching faculty in universities.)[5]

If an engineering department or school in a major university has never had a female faculty member, does that university have a "deficiency" and can it be charged with "excluding women"? If it should attract a female faculty member to its engineering school from another major institution by an offer at the same rank, has the university overcome its guilt? Can the university from which the female professor was attracted now be charged with sex discrimination for not having a female member in its engineering faculty, whereas formerly it did have one? Such questions assume undue significance under a system of government regulation that stresses numerical hiring goals.

If the supply of women who are well qualified for faculty positions in engineering is not increased but is only shifted from one university to another, what has been accomplished with respect to sex discrimination in universities beyond, perhaps, bidding up women's salaries, even above those for comparable men? It seems evident that the most effective affirmative action that major universities could take is not to bid the few qualified female engineers

[5] See Dodge (1966, pp. 137, 208, 279).

away from each other in a kind of game of musical chairs but to adopt effective measures to help increase the qualified supply.[6]

Unfortunately, important aspects of supply are neglected in the U.S. Department of Health, Education, and Welfare's *Higher Education Guidelines*[7] (Office for Civil Rights, 1972), issued for determining discrimination and for formulating affirmative action plans. In the HEW Guidelines, a university is given no credit whatsoever for affirmative action through successful efforts in expanding qualified supply; instead a university gets its required numerical goal for employing female faculty increased in proportion to the increase in supply that it achieves.[8]

THE SUPPLY AND DEMAND SIDES

Major universities can discriminate against women for faculty appointment and advancement on the supply side—in graduate education or in postgraduate training as a faculty colleague—or on the demand side—as employers of women who have the graduate training and acquire on-the-job training on their faculties. The supply and demand sides are, of course, in some respects closely interconnected.[9] It is, however, desirable to consider first and separately some of the ways that universities may discriminate against women in training and developing supply qualified for the different levels of teaching and research in higher education.

Universities may discriminate against women in admissions as undergraduate and graduate students. Especially at the graduate level, faculty play a primary part in making decisions on admission and fellowship or research support. Any limitations on female stu-

[6] Relative increases in women's salaries would, of course, tend to stimulate efforts to increase the qualified supply while at the same time encouraging economy in the use of women at the relatively higher salaries.

[7] Hereafter referred to as HEW Guidelines.

[8] The pertinent provision is as follows: "To the extent that an institution makes a practice of employing its own graduates [presumably in any department], the number and percentage of graduate degrees which it has itself awarded to women and minorities in the past ten years or so should be reflected in the goals it sets for its future faculty appointments" (Office for Civil Rights, 1972, p. J4). Most major universities would employ one or more Ph.D. candidates or recipients on the faculty at least for a short period of time.

[9] The supply and demand sides are interconnected, for example, because increased demand tends to stimulate the development of more qualified supply, and because, during his or her probationary, pretenure period on the faculty, the individual is acquiring generally valuable training in the profession to qualify for a tenure appointment, while at the same time engaging in regular full-time employment.

dents that are not placed on male students deny the former equal opportunity to qualify for professional careers, including careers as university faculty members. The same can be said with respect to scholarship and fellowship support.

More subtle is whether a department's faculty, in allocating fellowship or research support, discriminates against women if it takes any account of the fact that female students generally have a longer period of graduate study and complete their Ph.D. requirements at a later age than men. Data for the 1950s and 1960s show that consistently for each discipline there is a difference between the median ages of men and women at Ph.D. attainment; the average of all disciplines shows women to be two to three years older. Family responsibilities as wives and mothers are a significant factor causing the period of graduate study to be more prolonged for women, so that the average lapse of time between the baccalaureate and the doctoral degree was approximately 12 years in the case of 1,547 women who earned Ph.D. degrees in 1957 and 1958 (see Astin, 1969, pp. 19–20, 140–142, and the references therein).

Also, female graduate students are more likely to interrupt or discontinue their graduate study. A study of 3,542 recipients of Woodrow Wilson National Fellowships for preparation for an academic career (all of them at about the same level of intellectual ability and over a quarter of them women), who entered graduate school in 1958, 1959, and 1960, showed that only 18 percent of the women and 42 percent of the men had received Ph.D. degrees by mid-1966.[10] On the other hand, during the same period, 60 percent of the women and 36 percent of the men acquired master's degrees which, the author points out, may have been an adequate degree for the teaching career that many of the women then planned.

Do the facts that, on the average, women take longer to obtain a Ph.D. degree and that highly talented women have a higher dropout rate from graduate study than men have a prejudicial effect on their employment as faculty members in major universities? Presumably they can, unless there is insistence that selection must be made strictly on the basis of each individual's record and promise, apart from any group probabilities or average experience. And, as previously noted, it may be worth taking some risk on such

[10] The percentages are standardized for distribution by academic discipline since the average time to the Ph.D. is relatively short for the sciences and long for the humanities (Mooney, 1968).

scores where there is a distinct possibility that the candidate could become a distinguished member of the profession.

Marked fluctuations have occurred over the past half century in the number of doctor of philosophy degrees granted to women compared with men. Table 1 shows by five-year periods the percentage of the total Ph.D. degrees awarded by United States universities from 1920 through 1972 that were earned by women. The percentage for 1945 to 1949 is relatively high, not because the number of doctorates granted to women rose so much but because the number granted to men was so low from 1943 through 1947 as a result of the interruption of men's graduate study during World War II.

As Table I indicates, a drive for advanced study and high professional achievement characterized the generation of women who came of age in the 1920s and 1930s (President's Commission on the Status of Women, 1963, pp. 67–70). That drive slacked off after World War II to be replaced to a significant extent by women's interest in the home and care for young children during the years that are so crucial for preparing and establishing oneself in a professional academic career aimed at high achievement, namely, the years from 25 to 35.

The 1950s and early 1960s were years of "the baby boom." Between 1940 and 1965, the proportion of married women in the female population rose significantly, and the percentage of married

TABLE 1 ***Percentage of all Ph.D.'s granted between 1920 and 1972 that were received by women***

*Period**	*Percent*
1920–1924	15.2
1925–1929	15.2
1930–1934	14.7
1935–1939	14.8
1940–1944	13.9
1945–1949	15.1
1950–1954	9.4
1955–1959	10.5
1960–1964	10.8
1965–1969	12.1
1970–1972	14.9
All 52 years	12.6

* From 1920 to 1957 on a calendar-year basis; thereafter on a fiscal-year basis.

SOURCE: National Research Council, Office of Scientific Personnel, doctorate records file.

women in the age group 25 to 35 who had children under six years of age also increased markedly (see Bowen & Finegan, pp. 202–203 and Appendix Table 7-B, p. 586). Those developments helped to cause the labor force participation rates of these women to decline appreciably and to limit their career ambitions. A result was that in the 1950s and early 1960s a much smaller percentage of women both prepared themselves with Ph.D. training and drove hard to reach the top in their profession.

By the late 1960s and early 1970s, the demographic trends had changed. The proportion of women who were married had declined slightly, the percentage of married women with children under six years of age had dropped sharply, and the labor force participation of women aged 25 to 35 had risen. A new career-oriented drive was in full swing. There was more sharing of household duties among young couples, and stress was being put on the importance of married women having time to pursue academic careers. Generational changes in women's ambitions and the possibilities of fulfilling them through professional careers need to be taken into account, along with factors on the demand side, in any assessment of responsibility for "underrepresentation" of women among tenured faculty, especially in major universities.

Studies and statistics indicate that, in the past, the most serious obstacle to female faculty members progressing in their careers is marriage and children. That is the case even though about half of the female faculty in universities are not married,[11] and surveys indicate that female Ph.D.'s who are married are twice as likely to be childless as women in the same age group in the general population and that they are likely to have a smaller family if they do have children.[12]

[11] In a 1972–73 survey, 48 percent of the women in universities and the same percentage in all institutions of higher education had "no spouse" at the time (Bayer, 1973, p. 31).

In a survey of women who received Ph.D. degrees in the calendar years 1957 and 1958, it was found that seven or eight years later (December 1965 or early 1966), 55 percent were married or had been married, compared with a figure of 94 percent for women of comparable age in the general population (Astin, 1969, p. 27).

[12] The survey reported in Astin (1969, pp. 29–30) showed that 28 percent of the married women who had doctorates were childless at that time (that is, generally in their early forties) and that those with children had an average of 2.0 compared with 2.6 children for the women in their early forties in the general population. A survey of college and university faculty in 1968–69 showed that 40 percent of the women in university faculties had not married and that 67 percent had no children (Bayer, 1970, p. 12).

In a questionnaire survey sent out at the end of 1965, the women who received Ph.D. degrees in the calendar years 1957 and 1958 were asked about the problems they "encounter in developing [their] careers fully."[13] Eighty percent of them were then employed in academic institutions. The respondents were asked to indicate whether each item considered to be a career obstacle was a "major problem" or a "minor problem." In reply, 18 percent said that "finding adequate help at home" was a major problem, and 22 percent more said that it was a minor problem. Half of the respondents used some sort of outside help for household work and child care. Nevertheless the female doctorates, as a group, spent an average of 10 hours a week on child care plus 18 hours a week on household tasks such as cooking, cleaning, and marketing, which meant a very large claim on the time and energy of half of the female Ph.D.'s who were married (Astin, 1969, pp. 97, 101–102, 147, and 178–179).

"Employer discrimination" was considered a major problem by 12 percent of the women who held doctorates and a minor problem for an additional 24 percent. "Husband's job mobility" and "husband's negative attitudes toward my working" were considered a major problem by 6 and 2 percent, and a minor problem by 8 and 4 percent, respectively, of all respondents. Since only half of the respondents had husbands, those figures would need to be doubled for married women. Almost half of the female Ph.D.'s (45 percent) had been with the same employer during the seven or eight years since receiving their degrees, and half of the married women reported their husbands also had Ph.D. degrees (ibid., pp. 28, 102–103, and 179). If the husband moves to a new position that necessitates a change of employment for the wife, her employment opportunity and progress in her career can be adversely affected.

With respect to discrimination in employment, the female Ph.D.'s were asked: "If you have [presumably at any time] experienced any employment discrimination practices indicate which kind," with the choices listed in order of frequency of respondent designation, as follows: "differential salaries for men and women with the same training and experience" (40 percent of respondents); "differential sex policies regarding tenure, seniority, and promotions" (33 percent); "unwillingness and reservation on the part of employer to

[13] Astin (1969). A total of 1,547 complete questionnaires were returned for an 83 percent response.

designate administrative responsibility and authority to professional women employees" (33 percent); "employer prejudices against hiring a woman" (25 percent), and "other" (12 percent).[14]

With male faculty outnumbering female faculty in universities 6 to 1, many women cannot help but feel that their interests and problems are not given proper consideration by their departmental colleagues, by university appointments committees, and by the administration. With such a sex ratio, faculty personnel policies could be expected to be oriented toward the normal career patterns of males and to neglect, to some extent at least, the interests of women pursuing careers in academe. Until sex discrimination in employment was banned by federal Executive orders and legislation, and women's groups pressured for policies oriented toward women's needs, universities generally paid little attention to possible sex bias in their hiring and employment policies. For example, antinepotism policies, either stated or assumed, served to reduce married women's employment opportunities by making it difficult for a female Ph.D. to obtain appropriate employment in the same university faculty as her husband, or to obtain part-time employment in regular faculty ranks, with all the leave-of-absence, benefit, and tenure rights and privileges that males on part-time status would have. Female faculty especially need those provisions for periods when pregnancy and child-rearing may make part-time employment necessary and desirable. Undoubtedly, scholars who aim at freedom from bias in their scholarly and scientific work should be reminded of the need to have fairness and equality of opportunity in the content and administration of university personnel policies.

It is interesting that statistics indicate that single women on university faculties seem notably less disadvantaged than married women. Undoubtedly that is due in large part to the handicaps that married women have in running a home and in adjusting to their husband's job mobility, both of which have already been discussed.[15]

[14] Ibid. (p. 179). Since male faculty members may also consider themselves discriminated against in salary, promotion, and distribution of administrative responsibility and authority, it would be interesting to have the response of a similar cohort of male Ph.D.'s to the same questions.

[15] As indicated in the text, the December 1965 survey of women receiving Ph.D.'s in 1957 and 1958 showed that about one-fourth of the married women considered their husband's job mobility a hindrance to their own career development, and for a sixth of them their husband's attitude toward their working was

Some studies indicate that marital status is perhaps the most significant factor in explaining differences in salary and in promotion rates between women and men. An analysis of the faculty status of women and men in the cohort who received Ph.D. degrees in 1940 and remained in academic employment shows that 20 years later (in 1960) some 85 percent of the males and 70 percent of the unmarried women had attained the rank full professor, whereas only 46 percent of the married women had done so. It was concluded that about three-fifths of the promotion differential between women and men academics in that sample could be explained by comparing single women with men.[16]

A questionnaire survey in 1967 of women who received their Ph.D.'s in the arts and sciences and education between 1958 and 1963, and who were employed full-time in faculty positions, had similar results. Among the unmarried women in 1966–67, the ratio of instructors and assistant professors combined (the first rungs on the promotional ladder) to associate and full professors combined was as follows: for single women, 1.1 full and associate professors for each instructor assistant professor; for men, 1.3 full and associate professors per instructor–assistant professor; and for married women, 0.4 of a full and associate professor per instructor-assistant professor (Simon, Clark, & Galway, 1967, p. 226).[17] The figures for percentages on tenure were much the same: 44 percent for single women, 46 percent for men, 26 percent for married women with children, and 22 percent for married women without children (ibid., p. 229). The view has been expressed that radical reform in sex roles and in responsibilities for household functions and child-rearing will be necessary to provide married women an equal opportunity with men to advance in their professional careers. As already noted, a significant increase in the sharing of such duties has occurred among some young couples in academic life in recent years.

---

regarded as a hindrance. The married women were presumably spending an average of around 20 hours a week on the care of children (the 10-hour figure was an average for all women) plus the 18-hour-a-week average for all women spent on household duties.

[16] See Johnson and Stafford (forthcoming). This part of the paper is based on data from National Academy of Sciences (1968, pp. 21, 71, and 85). See also Malkiel and Malkiel (1973).

[17] Completed questionnaires were received from about 60 percent of the women and men (a sample one-third the size of the women's list), leaving an academic-employed sample of 670 single women, 148 married women, 234 married women with children, and 354 men.

Since World War II there has been a secular rise in the emphasis on research in faculty careers, especially in major universities. At the same time in many disciplines the rate of creation of new knowledge has been accelerating. Those developments require more preparation to keep abreast of changes and the allocation of more faculty time to research activity. It becomes increasingly difficult for a woman with heavy household responsibilities to make an outstanding record as a scholar or even to keep abreast of developments in her field.

Data on teaching faculty in universities show that women generally devote much less time to research activities and do less graduate teaching than men. To some extent the figures are biased against female faculty because of the high proportion of female Ph.D.'s in education and home economics, where research is likely to receive less stress. Even allowing for that fact, the male-female differences are significant.

A survey for 1972–73 reveals the following facts concerning teaching faculty in universities: the highest degree held is the Ph.D. or Ed.D. for 19 percent of the women and 48 percent of the men; while the M.A. is the highest degree for 60 percent of the women and 25 percent of the men;[18] 42 percent of the women and 19 percent of the men spend no time in research and scholarly writing (or did not answer the question); at the other extreme, 9 percent of the women and 24 percent of the men spend 17 hours a week or more in such research activities. Ten percent of the women and 39 percent of the men had published 11 or more journal articles, and 11 percent of the women and 24 percent of the men had published three or more books, manuals, or monographs. Concerning published writings in the most recent two years, 14 percent of the women and 40 percent of the men had three or more publications during that period. Thirteen percent of the women and 25 percent of the men considered that their single most outstanding accomplishment was in research and writing. With respect to graduate students, 49 percent of the female faculty and 31 percent of the men currently were not teaching any graduate students.[19]

[18] Bayer (1973, p. 26). Of the remainder, 5 percent of the women and 9 percent of the men have professional law or medical degrees.

[19] Ibid. (pp. 24, 28–29, and 32). The category of "none" for teaching of graduate students includes respondents not marking that part of the question but pro-

No clear conclusions can be drawn from the available data on the relative importance of the various obstacles to the development of a larger supply of women who could in the future, through research and advanced teaching, qualify for tenure positions in major universities, if equal employment opportunity were assured women aiming at top-rank faculty careers. It is even difficult to define exactly what nondiscrimination and equal employment opportunity mean, given the complexity of the factors and considerations involved. Nevertheless it is evident that talented women, by the choices they make and the priority they give to career ambitions, can have a significant effect on the supply of women able to qualify for tenure faculty appointments at major universities.

EXPERIENCE IN WESTERN EUROPE AND RUSSIA

Marked differences exist in the distribution of men and the distribution of women by faculty rank in universities in both this country and abroad. For male faculty, the largest number are at the professor level; for female faculty, the largest number are at the assistant professor level. The distribution for female faculty is shaped like a pyramid; the male faculty distribution is shaped like an inverted pyramid. The contrast is brought out in Table 2 showing the overall figures for university faculties in the United States in the academic year 1972–73. Two-thirds of the male faculty are

TABLE 2 ***Percentage distribution of university faculty by rank and sex for the United States, 1972–73***

Rank	*Men*	*Women*
Professor	41	12
Associate professor	26	20
Assistant professor	22	35
Instructor	6	23
*Other rank, including lecturer**	5	9
TOTAL	100	100

* "Other rank" includes one-half of 1 percent who lack a rank designation.

NOTE: For women, the figures do not total 100 due to rounding.

SOURCE: Bayer (1973, p. 23).

viding answers to other parts and to other questions, thus providing grounds for believing that the percentages in the text are approximately correct. The survey of college and university faculty conducted in 1968–69 by Bayer showed that 48 percent of the female faculty in universities and 24 percent of the men were teaching entirely in undergraduate programs.

TABLE 3 ***Women and men in university faculties as percentage of total in the rank, 1972–73***

Rank	*Women*	*Men*
Professor	5.2	94.8
Associate professor	12.3	87.7
Assistant professor	22.2	77.8
Instructor and lecturer	37.6	62.4
TOTAL	15.3	84.7

SOURCE: Bayer (1973, pp. 8, 11, 23). The 1.6 percent of faculty without rank or having some other rank are omitted from the table.

in the two tenure ranks (professor and associate professor), whereas only one-third of the female faculty have that status.[20]

Table 3 shows the marked difference in the proportion of women and men in the various ranks. The women's percentages are progressively smaller as one moves up in rank. The male percentages—the obverse of the female—have the inverted pyramid shape, expanding in percentage terms with each higher rank.

It is widely asserted that any significant deviation of the women's distribution in the three professorial ranks from the men's distribution in those ranks is evidence of a pattern of sex discrimination. The assumption is that equal employment opportunity would lead to the same percentage for women in each professional rank. That assumption fails to take account of the distribution of the qualified supply of women for university appointment at particular ranks. Because, on the average, female faculty devote less time and energy to professional development (especially research) than men and more time to home responsibilities, a smaller percentage of women really qualify for the upper ranks.

Two kinds of factual information support that conclusion. One is that the distribution of single women by faculty rank seems, as we have observed, to resemble the distribution for men more than it does the distribution for married women. The other is that the difference between male and female distributions for university faculty appears to be a generally prevalent phenomenon.

It is remarkable how universal the pyramid shape of women's distribution in the academic profession is. In her useful review of experience of women at work in European countries, Marjorie Galenson finds that, in university teaching in every country for which data are available, the percentages become smaller as one

[20] The age distribution of male and female faculty is quite similar except that 11 percent of the women and only 5 percent of the men are in the category of "30 or less."

moves up the promotional ladder, with relatively few women at the full professor level (Galenson, 1973, pp. 27, 107–108). She observes that it is "an apparently universal phenomenon" with the professions for the proportion of women to decline "as the promotional ladder is ascended." As part of the explanation she points out that "unlike single women, who are likely, other things equal, to be more successful over their working lives, the probability is that married women will continue to subordinate their careers to their major commitment to their families for a long time to come" (ibid., p. 112).

The experience of the Soviet Union is most instructive in this regard, and shows how basic the pyramid distribution for faculty women is.[21] For decades Russian women have enjoyed equal employment opportunity under a strong government and Communist party affirmative action plan. The Soviet Union appears to lead the world in making use of the creative talents of women in fields that elsewhere are dominated by men. For example, women constitute three-quarters of the medical profession, one-half of the scientific workers in research institutions, and one-third of the engineers in the country (Dodge, 1966, pp. 193–95, 211, 237).

In education and advanced training for professional careers, there has been practically no differentiation by sex. A uniform curriculum through the tenth grade ensures that girls will receive as much training in science and mathematics as boys. For many decades there has been free and equal access to university and professional training and free choice of the field of study and of occupation. Soon after the Soviets came into power, basic legislation was passed providing sexual equality of employment opportunity.

Compared with other countries, the Soviets have been remarkably successful in interesting women in fields of science, technology, and medicine. In recent decades, the national government has made major efforts, through the mass media, to interest girls and young women in professional careers and to gain social approval for women in professional work as intelligent and patriotic citizens. Such efforts have been generally successful. By 1947, women

[21] Professor Norton T. Dodge has made a thorough study of academic training of women in the Soviet Union for professional occupations and of women's achievements particularly in science and technology in universities and research institutes. His analysis covers the period from the Revolution (1917) to 1966, when his book on the subject was published. This discussion of women in teaching and research in Soviet universities is based on Dodge's book.

constituted 35 percent of the teaching staffs of institutions of higher education. They were 47 percent of the teachers of biology and medicine, 45 percent of the chemists, 23 percent of the geologists, and 21 percent of the physicists and mathematicians (ibid., p. 244). Between 1946 and 1964 women received about 30 percent of the Ph.D.'s (equivalent) that were granted (ibid., pp. 136–137).[22]

Despite the Soviet Union's success in encouraging women to pursue professional careers, the pyramid phenomenon prevails. As Table 4 shows, women constitute a decreasing percentage of those in the rank as one moves up from assistant professor to professor. The greatest differential between the sexes is at highest levels of scholarly and scientific achievement (ibid., pp. 236–245).[23]

Professor Dodge explains that Soviet women, who have the training and capacity for first-rank creative work in the arts and

[22] The Ph.D. equivalent is called the "candidate degree." It may be earned through completion of formal training, with examinations and defense of a dissertation, or on a merit basis as recognition for outstanding scholarly or scientific work without examinations or a thesis defense. Formal work toward the candidate degree may be done at regular universities and technical institutes or at scientific research institutes or laboratories. Women constituted about 30 percent of those holding candidate degrees in 1965 (Dodge, 1966, pp. 134, 199).

[23] It should be pointed out that the Russian figures are not strictly comparable with those for the United States. In Russia, persons once certified in an advanced academic rank (professor, associate professor) continue to retain that rank in the statistics wherever he or she is employed—in universities, research establishments, industry, or government. About two-thirds of the professors of both sexes are employed in universities, and it can be assumed that practically all of them have Ph.D. equivalency since three-fourths have the even more advanced "doctor degree." Almost three-fourths of the associate professors are employed in institutions of higher education, and over 90 percent of them have the equivalent of the Ph.D. (the candidate degree). The bulk of the junior research workers are in scientific research establishments and the majority of assistant professors are in institutions of higher education; of this combined group less than one-quarter have the candidate degree.

TABLE 4
Female scientific workers with academic titles in the Soviet Union; percentage distribution by rank and percentage of total in the rank, 1964

	Distribution	*Percent of rank*
Academicians, corresponding members, and professors	2.3	8.3
Associate professors	20.5	19.1
Senior research workers	18.4	29.0
Junior research workers and assistant professors	58.7	52.3
Total (or percent of total)	100.0	32.2

SOURCE: Dodge (1966, p. 197).

sciences, generally have a lower level of achievement than men because child-care and household duties do not permit the sustained intellectual concentration that such achievement requires (ibid., p. 233)[24] He found from an extensive analysis of articles in scientific and technical journals, "further unmistakable evidence that the scholarly productivity of women is lower than that of men"; the analysis showed that "the average woman contributed about half as many articles as would be expected from their numbers" in the academic discipline.[25] Although the career obstacles of marriage and motherhood are not likely to be reduced drastically in the future, Dodge believes that probably the "professional productivity" of women is likely to increase over the years as their potential for creative work is more fully realized, which, in turn, would lead to a higher proportion of women in the upper ranks of the universities and technical institutes (ibid., p. 236).[26]

That there now is a good basis for such a conclusion is indicated by Table 5. Although progress has not been rapid from 1950 to 1970, there is an unmistakable upward trend in the percentages for full and associate professors relative to those for research workers and assistant professors, as well as an overall increase in the percentage of female faculty.[27] To that extent the extreme triangle has been modified in the Soviet Union.

[24] Dodge concludes (1966, p. 4) "that the relatively small proportion of women in jobs with the greatest responsibility is far more a reflection of their lower productivity than the result of discrimination."

In the mid-1960s, it was estimated that approximately 12 percent of the children of nursery age and 20 percent of the children of kindergarten age were accommodated in permanent child-care facilities, mostly in urban centers. Women's liberation from housework had partly taken place through sharing of that work. Data for certain cities in the early 1960s indicated that men were spending two-thirds as much time as their working wives on household duties and child care. Nevertheless, working mothers generally continued to bear a disproportionate burden compared with men (ibid., pp. 94, 98).

[25] See Dodge (ibid., pp. 236, 245, and 304–305), where the method used by the author in making the analysis of publications by sex is explained.

[26] Dodge points out that the personal contacts among male scientists going back to the 1920s and 1930s, when female scientists were less plentiful, may be a factor in the continued male dominance of the highest echelons of the scientific academies (ibid., pp. 220–222).

[27] It should be pointed out that the percentages in Table 5 are undoubtedly somewhat affected by a high woman-man ratio and a high proportion of single women that existed during this period as a result of so many men being killed in World War I, the Revolution, and especially World War II. The ratio of men to women in the Russian population fell from 99 men to 100 women in 1897 to 92 in 1939 and 74 in 1946, and had risen to 83 by 1959 (ibid., p. 238).

TABLE 5 ***Women as a percentage in each rank according to academic titles, Soviet Union, 1950, 1960, 1965, and 1970***

Titles	*1950*	*1960*	*1965*	*1970*
Academicians, corresponding members, and professors	5.4	7.3	8.8	9.9
Associate professors	14.8	17.1	19.5	21.0
Senior research workers	30.4	28.4	28.9	25.1
Junior research workers and assistant professors	48.0	51.0	51.1	49.8
TOTAL	26.9	28.2	38.3	38.8

SOURCE: Dodge (1966, Table 115, pp. 196–197, updated by Dr. Dodge with data from *Narodnoe khoziaistvo SSSR v. 1969 godu* and *ibid. v. 1970 godu,* pp. 709–710 and 656–657). There are still lower categories not included among the figures in this table, which are the equivalent of instructors and teaching assistants.

This long experience in the Soviet Union indicates how unrealistic the statement (page J4 in the HEW Guidelines) concerning the timetable for achieving the HEW goal of proportional representation for female faculty is: "In many cases this [overcoming all underrepresentation] can be accomplished within 5 years; in others more time or less time will be required." That statement is made at a time when 65 percent of the regular university faculty have tenure and the total university faculty is not growing and is not expected to expand much in the next 5 years.

THE SITUATION FOR BLACK FACULTY

The supply situation for black men and women for university teaching differs significantly from that for white women. Women in general represent around 13 percent of all holders of Ph.D. degrees; blacks of both sexes constitute about 1 percent of those with Ph.D. degrees.[28]

A survey in 1969 revealed that of the 1,096 blacks with Ph.D.'s who responded,[29] approximately four-fifths were men and one-fifth women. About three-quarters of them had received their undergraduate training in black colleges. Some 85 percent of the Ph.D. holders were in college and university teaching, and of those on faculties, four-fifths were holding positions in Negro colleges (ibid., pp. 4, 7–8).

[28] A survey in 1968–69 indicated that less than 1 percent of all earned doctoral degrees in this country are held by blacks. In the five years from 1964 through 1968, black Americans received 0.8 percent of the Ph.D.'s awarded by graduate schools of arts and sciences in this country. See Bryant (1969, pp. 3 and 7).

[29] The survey had the names of 2,280 black Ph.D.'s from whom 1,096 questionnaire replies were received, or about a 50 percent return.

The survey found that, as generally has been the case for women, it required a longer period for blacks to complete their Ph.D. training—their median period for completion was 13 years. The average age at which they obtained the Ph.D. degree was around 37 years. The black Ph.D.'s were distributed as follows: 29 percent in education, 26 percent in the social sciences, 25 percent in the biological and physical sciences, 12 percent in the humanities, and the remaining 8 percent in other fields such as agriculture, business, engineering, home economics, and religion.[30]

As such data indicate, black Ph.D.'s in academic careers have, generally speaking, been disadvantaged (1) by shortcomings in their educational preparation before entering graduate school and (2) by lack of sufficient opportunity to make important research contributions because such a large proportion of them are in college teaching, especially at Negro colleges where the stress has had to be primarily on teaching.

Universities can undoubtedly make their greatest affirmative action contribution on the supply side by exerting strong efforts to encourage able black students to enter on an academic career, to assist them in getting excellent professional training in graduate school and in completing their Ph.D. requirements as soon as feasible, and to help in getting them started on an important program of research in the early years after they obtain their Ph.D. degrees. In recent years, major universities have been engaged in such efforts.

From 1968 on, many universities have made strong efforts to develop and acquire black faculty. With the launching of Afro-American studies programs or departments in the late 1960s, staffed largely by blacks, and under pressure from HEW compliance officials and black students, a kind of special market tended to develop for black faculty. Many universities offered appointments to black faculty at salaries well above those for whites with equivalent or better qualifications. In some cases the salary offers were $3,000 to $4,000 a year higher for blacks at the assistant professor level and $5,000 to $8,000 higher at the associate and full professor levels.[31]

[30] See Bryant (1969, pp. 5–6). The average age upon receipt of the Ph.D. was calculated from Table II, p. 6.

[31] Among the most extreme instances of reverse discrimination were the offer of associate professorships to blacks just completing their Ph.D.'s and the case of a black assistant professor of philosophy on full-time appointment at a yearly salary of $13,000 at Yale in 1971–72, who was discovered to have also a full-time tenure appointment at the New York State University at Stony Brook at double the salary—$26,000 (*New York Times,* 1972).

As early as 1968 a significant increase had occurred in the number of job inquiries and job offers received by black faculty. A study, based on a sample of 699 black faculty in some 184 non-Southern, predominantly white colleges and on a comparable sample of 440 white faculty (40 percent of the blacks and 70 percent of the whites had Ph.D. degrees), showed that for the academic year 1968–69 the blacks averaged 3.1 job offers, whereas the whites averaged 1.5 offers. The author states that "Blacks with the doctorate from high quality schools who have published report jobs by invitation almost four times as often as whites with the same excellent credentials" and that as early as 1968–69 there was "reverse discrimination in which blacks already in the academic profession are sought out by predominantly white colleges and universities" (Rafky, 1971).

A questionnaire study in 1970, answered by 1,385 blacks with Ph.D. degrees, indicated that the median increase in salary necessary to attract them away from their present positions (mostly in predominantly black institutions) was around $7,500 a year in biological sciences, $6,250 in the social sciences, and $5,500 in the physical sciences and humanities (Mommsen, forthcoming). Such salary elevations would represent a median increase from existing salaries amounting to around 45 percent for those in biological sciences and roughly 35 percent in the other three divisions. Since the black Ph.D.'s had reported increasing numbers of job inquiries and offers during the previous academic year, there was some factual basis for their supply-price figures. Also, their responses indicated that generally they would be more influenced by career opportunities at institutions from which they might receive offers than they would by the racial composition of the faculties.

As the percentages in Table 6 indicate, the expansion in black faculty during that four-year period was heavily concentrated in universities, where their proportion of total faculty almost doubled, and in two-year colleges, where their proportion tripled. The four-year colleges, including the Negro colleges, showed only a small

TABLE 6 ***Black faculty as a percentage of total college and university faculty in the United States, 1968–69 and 1972–73***

Type of institution	*1968–69*	*1972–73*
Universities	0.5	0.9
Four-year colleges	5.0	5.4
Two-year colleges	0.7	2.1
All institutions	2.2	2.9

SOURCES: Bayer (1970, p. 12) and Bayer (1973, p. 31).

increase. The most rapid expansions were for men in universities (0.4 to 0.9 percent; women, only 1.0 to 1.2 percent) and for women and men in two-year colleges (women, 1.4 to 4.2 percent; men, 0.5 to 1.3 percent).[32]

The corresponding figures for women are significantly different, as Table 7 indicates. Women declined as a percentage of the faculty in four-year colleges and in two-year colleges from 1968–69 to 1972–73. Only universities showed a relative increase in female faculty in that four year period, which raised the women's percentage of total faculty from 19 to 20 percent.

STATISTICAL ANALYSES OF SEX BIAS IN SALARIES

Universities are charged also with discrimination against women in terms of salary. This section critically examines three statistical studies of sex differentials in faculty salaries, drawing also on material already presented in this chapter. Two of the studies, one by Elizabeth Scott (Carnegie Commission, 1973*b,* pp. 115–123 and Appendix E, pp. 199–235) and the other by Helen S. Astin and Alan E. Bayer (1973, pp. 333–356) use the Carnegie Commission Survey of Faculty and Student Opinion (1969 data)[33] as the statistical basis for their analyses and conclusions. The study by George E. Johnson and Frank P. Stafford (forthcoming)[34] primarily uses National Science Foundation data for

[32] It is interesting to note, by way of contrast, that the percentages for Asian faculty between 1968–69 and 1972–73 remained fairly constant (except for a significant increase in two-year colleges), so that for all institutions the percentages were 1.3 percent in 1968–69 and 1.5 percent in 1972–73.

[33] Faculty material in that survey is contained in Alan E. Bayer (1970), to which reference is made in Tables 6 and 7 and in footnotes in this chapter. Scott used a selected sample of 17,654 and Astin and Bayer a sample of 6,892, out of a nationally representative sample of 460,028 faculty members in 253 institutions.

[34] Johnson and Stafford's paper is part of a project on academic and professional compensation sponsored by the American Association of University Professors. See "Surviving the Seventies" (1973).

TABLE 7 ***Female faculty as a percentage of total college and university faculty in the United States, 1968–69 and 1972–73***

Type of institution	*1968–69*	*1972–73*
Universities	14.8	16.5
Four-year colleges	22.7	21.8
Two-year colleges	25.6	21.9
All institutions	19.1	20.0

SOURCES: Bayer (1970, p. 7) and Bayer (1973, p. 11).

Ph.D.'s in academic employment in six disciplines. Its analysis applies life-cycle training theory, which, starting with a little sex difference at the time of completion of the Ph.D., analyzes sex differences in salary thereafter in terms of on-the-job training or development of professional earning capacity (human capital) during the individual's ensuing life cycle over a 30-year period.

Statistical studies of discrimination in employment are handicapped by the fact that discrimination is not directly measurable. Thus its association with a particular factor or factors cannot be directly calculated. Instead, a residual approach is often used. Allowance is made for the calculated effect of each of a number of relevant factors, and any remaining difference (residual quantity) after such allowance is assumed to represent discrimination.

The residual approach for determining discrimination in employment is likely to be plagued by two difficulties. The first is that one or more significant factors (variables) may be left out of the analysis, which will, of course, affect the size of the residual. The second difficulty involves determination of the amount by which each individual's stock of "human capital" (earning power) is enhanced through his or her on-the-job experience (teaching, research, and learning from colleagues). Spread of a certain quantity of experience over a longer period of time for women than for men, due to part-time service or gaps in employment, may result in a smaller net increase in women's earning power through on-the-job experience. Partly that may be because of the time factor in obsolescence of knowledge and skills in fast-moving fields. Obviously, unless adequate allowance is made for such factors, at least part of any residual should not be attributed to discrimination.

The Scott study is a macro-type analysis in that it uses statistics representing all colleges and universities, including professional schools, in quite broad categories. The analysis is broken down for arts and sciences only by division (biological and physical sciences, social sciences, humanities, and fine arts) and by the six Carnegie Commission classifications of colleges and universities (Research Universities I, Research Universities II and other Doctoral-Granting Universities I and II, Comprehensive Universities and Colleges, etc.)[35] There is no breakdown by

[35] Research Universities I are the 50 leading universities in terms of federal financial support of academic science in two of three years, which awarded at least 50 Ph.D's in 1969–70. Research Universities II and other Doctoral-

faculty rank, by academic department, or by individual institution.

Essentially the Scott study employs a complex statistical analysis (multiple-regression analysis) for arriving at predicted salaries for men and women on the basis of the data. The analysis involves taking into account the influence of 30 variables—personal characteristics, education, experience, and institution—that are associated with differences in faculty members' salaries. Among the 30 predictor variables are age, highest academic degree, year degree was obtained, prestige of granting institution, years employed in higher education, years employed in present institution, scheduled hours of teaching per week, number of published articles, and number of published books.

A predicted average salary was calculated after statistically controlling for all 30 predictor variables in a multiple-regression equation. A separate analysis is made for men and for women, since some of the coefficients for particular variables are significantly different for men and women. For example, advanced degrees are calculated to be much more significant salarywise for men than for women; the coefficients show that, for men, salaries vary directly with the quality of the employing institution within each category of institution, and not for women; but the effect of the number of publications on salary was determined to be about the same for both sexes (Carnegie Commission, 1973*b*, pp. 206–207).[36]

On the basis of the female regression equation, the predicted average salary for male faculty members for all institutions is found to be below the average of their actual salaries by $2,264 a year; for Research Universities I that predicted-actual differential is $2,729. On the basis of the male regression equation, the predicted average for female faculty in all institutions is

Granting Universities I and II are three categories that awarded at least 50, 40, and 10 Ph.D's, respectively, in 1969–70, and in the case of Research Universities II are on the list of the 100 leading institutions in terms of federal financial support. The three categories total 121 institutions. Comprehensive Universities and Colleges I and II are 453 institutions that offer liberal arts programs, have one or more professional or occupational programs, and may offer master's degrees. For more detail on these categories see Carnegie Commission (1973*a*).

[36] It is interesting to observe that the Astin and Bayer study (1973, pp. 350–351), using the same 1969 data and similar statistical methods, seems to contradict these conclusions with respect to the significance of the three variables as stated in the text.

$1,407 above the actual salary; for Research Universities I, the predicted average for women is $2,009 above the actual average. The predicted-actual differences are largest in dollar terms for Research Universities I of any of the six categories of institutions and are smallest for Comprehensive Universities and Colleges. Indeed, for Research Universities I for the biological and physical sciences, the difference between the predicted and actual average salaries is most surprising. In those sciences, a great majority of the male faculty received salaries in 1969 that ranged roughly from $1,000 to $7,500 above the predicted salaries on the basis of the female regression equation, and slightly under 10 percent of the male faculty in those sciences received salaries $10,000 to $13,000 above the predicted amounts (Carnegie Commission, 1973*b,* p. 116 and Chart 14, p. 117). In considering the magnitude of those differentials, one should bear in mind the average salary figures for university faculty in the 1968–69 salary survey of the American Association of University Professors; they ranged from an average of $10,534 for assistant professors to an average of $17,000 for full professors ("The Threat of Inflationary Erosion," 1969, Appendix Table 5, p. 208).

Questions can be raised about the validity of the predicted salaries themselves, and the soundness of their use for assessing actual responsibility for discrimination. Those aspects will be considered after attention is given to the Astin-Bayer study that uses the same basic data and similar methods of analysis.

Before considering the Astin-Bayer study it should be mentioned that Scott also compared differences in faculty salaries associated with race by a similar method. There was a slight tendency for the predicted average salary of black male faculty to be above the actual average, on the basis of the equation for all men, and a slight tendency for the predicted average salary of black women to be slightly below the average actual salary for female faculty, on the basis of the equation for all women. But the differences are not statistically significant (Carnegie Commission, 1973*b,* pp. 209 and 224).

The Astin-Bayer study uses multiple-regression analysis to predict salaries of male faculty compared with female faculty and also to make similar predictions with respect to academic rank and tenure. Instead of using the regression equation of the opposite sex, Astin and Bayer apply to the women's data the regression weights of the predictor variables calculated from the men's sample.

The difference between actual average salary and predicted average salary for women for the whole sample is $1,040—actual salary averaged that much less than predicted salary (Astin & Bayer, 1973, p. 353). The authors say that it is a minimum figure because the regression weights of the predictor variables for the male sample are used, and the result does not include salary discrimination attributable to discrimination in rank. Astin and Bayer do not provide breakdowns by disciplinary areas or type of institution.

With respect to both the Scott and Astin-Bayer studies it should be pointed out that the use of large numbers of predictor variables as a basis for judging the existence and extent of sex discrimination in salary is subject to serious weaknesses. Only quantifiable aspects of each variable are included in the analysis. Unmeasurable, quality aspects of teaching, research and publications, and administrative service, although usually important in determining an individual's "productivity," tend to be neglected. Scheduled teaching hours are not all equal, as Scott clearly recognizes. Successful teaching of advanced courses and lecturing to large numbers of undergraduates in a rapidly changing field are more demanding in terms of scarce competencies than teaching sections in an elementary course, year after year. The former is more likely to be done by men, the latter by women in some departments.

Qualitative differences that affect productivity can be illustrated by examples. In many universities, a significant part of the instruction in courses in non-Western languages is given by native-speaking persons, mostly women. Some of them may ultimately earn a Ph.D. degree but still be qualified mostly for language teaching and not for advanced courses in literature or history. Their teaching per hour cannot be considered equal to that of a distinguished professor in the literature or history of the country where that language is the native tongue. Also Astin and Bayer make no allowance for part-time as distinguished from full-time teaching although, for reasons indicated in the Johnson-Stafford paper, part-time service may have important implications for salary in future years.[37]

[37] Briefly, the reason is that inclusion in the analysis of part-time service years as years of experience can be misleading if the rest of the person's time while on part-time teaching was occupied with nonprofessional activities, which means a decline or interruption in the development of professional skills and reputation that influence "productivity" and earnings.

Furthermore, it is noteworthy that neither Scott nor Astin-Bayer compare the salaries of single women and male faculty. As already explained, the pattern of advancement in rank and salary for single women resembles that for men and presumably would show little sex differences in salary.

Certainly, one cannot assume that 30 predictor variables can serve to predict the average salary that women would be paid if there were no sex discrimination in salary determination on the part of institutions of higher education. The difference between the predicted average salary and the actual salary of female faculty in the two studies is in the nature of a residual still to be explained. At least part of that residual could be due to weaknesses in the predictor variables or to sex differences in productivity factors (e.g., career motivation, ability to perform demanding teaching assignments, standing in the discipline and the profession) not taken into account in the analysis.

It should be noted that analyses of faculty salaries by sex made in individual major universities, some in field investigations under the Federal Equal Pay Act, generally do not find a "pervasive pattern" of lower salaries for female faculty of the magnitude indicated by the Scott and Astin-Bayer calculations and especially by Scott's calculations for biological and physical sciences in major universities, where laboratory research contributions (often with graduate students) are such an important factor in academic reputation and in faculty salary determination. Faculty salary studies by individual institution (microeconomic case studies)[38] are likely to provide much more reliable results than macro-type analyses based on the use of many predictor variables.

The Johnson-Stafford study analyzes factors that may explain much of the differential in faculty salaries between men and women. Their analysis is based mainly on data from the National Register of Scientific and Technical Personnel for 1970.[39] Six disciplines are chosen for particular examination. They are anthropology, biology, economics, mathematics, physics, and sociology.

Johnson and Stafford point out that salary data for the first

[38] For such a microeconomic case study, see Malkiel and Malkiel (1973).

[39] Source of data: Tapes of the National Register of Scientific and Technical Personnel, National Science Foundation.

academic appointment after completing the Ph.D. degree show comparatively small differences by sex in most of the disciplines. At that point, the average differential between men's and women's salaries in academia ranged from women's salaries 4 to 8 percent lower in five disciplines to 12 percent lower in biology.

For all six disciplines, the percentage differential between male and female salaries widens during the first 20 years of experience after acquiring the Ph.D. degree. During those 20 years, the sex differential widened for the six disciplines as follows: anthropology, 8 to 23 percent; biology, 11 to 26 percent; economics, 5 to 15 percent; mathematics, 6 to 26 percent; physics, 6 to 22 percent; and sociology, 4 to 14 percent. The salary differential widened most rapidly between the fifth and fifteenth years of postdoctoral and professional experience. Generally, during those 10 years the women were between 35 and 45 years of age, when they were most likely to have heavy household and child-care responsibilities.

Johnson and Stafford also made an analysis of salaries and experience of faculty members who, in 1972, were assistant, associate, and full professors at Michigan State University in the six disciplines. They found that the starting salaries for the female faculty in those disciplines averaged only 3 percent lower than corresponding salaries for male faculty, and that figure does not have much statistical significance. At 15 years of reported academic experience, the differential had grown to 20 percent, and thereafter it declined somewhat with more years of experience above 15.

The National Register data also show a narrowing of the sex differential in half of the six disciplines after a certain period of experience. Classifying experience by five-year intervals up to 30 years, the sex salary-differential is largest in percentage terms at 20 years for economics and physics, at 25 years for sociology, and at 30 years for anthropology, biology, and mathematics. In other words, in the first three disciplines the sex differential for salaries narrowed somewhat (1, 2, or 3 percentage points) after 20 or 25 years of experience; in the other three disciplines the sex differential continued to enlarge a few percentage points up to the thirtieth year of experience, the final year included in the analysis.

The changes in the size of the sex salary-differential over time are explained by Johnson and Stafford largely in terms of difference in time devoted to improving earning capacity—investment in "human capital." They point out that, at the time of completion of the Ph.D., the earning capacity and the learning ability of males and females are approximately equal, and so are their salaries. Thereafter, however, married women, in general, are not likely to devote as much time and effort to increasing their earning capacity and preventing its obsolescence as is generally the case for male faculty, especially during the first 15 years of their academic careers.

Two factors help to explain a significant divergence in women's capacity or "productivity" as teacher-scholars after starting with no apparent overall difference in career preparation and capacity at the point of Ph.D. completion. One is the individual's expectation that she will have a period when family obligations will necessarily cause some curtailment of time and effort that she can devote to professional development. That expectation tends to affect women's career aims, motivation, and planning. Two, a woman's job preferences and her stress on job components may favor teaching (drawing heavily on existing stock of "human capital" from previous training, which may experience significant obsolescence) and put less emphasis on research (that helps to develop and renew the teacher-scholar's capital, not only through the results of the research but also the process of interchange with teacher-scholars in the field concerning that research and research results of others in the field). Less time and effort are actually devoted to research and scholarship, which keep one intellectually alive and on top of one's subject, because so much time and attention, during a vital period for progress in one's profession, are taken up with family and household duties. Assessment of the value of the individual as a teacher-scholar by colleagues in the university and by persons in the discipline at other institutions is affected by a relative decline in the individual's "human capital" as a faculty member in the discipline. That is likely to influence recommendations for salary increase and promotion that are based on merit, and also the number and salary of outside job inquiries and offers.

The first 10 years after completing the Ph.D. requirements are especially important for progress in a career as a teacher-scholar in the arts and sciences. That is particularly true for laboratory sciences like the biological sciences, in which the reputation of teacher-scholars depends so heavily on instruction of advanced students in the laboratory and on the quality of one's research contributions. Competition is keen in those terms, and obsolescence of knowledge is quite rapid in most subject areas.

The Johnson-Stafford study indicates additional dangers in drawing conclusions about sex discrimination from cross-sectional studies that neglect differences in the rate of individual professional development over time. Studies of sex discrimination in university salaries and conclusions drawn from them about discrimination should take account of factors that influence the value of the individual as a teacher-scholar to the particular institution.

The material in this chapter shows the complications and pitfalls that attend attempts to calculate the amount of discrimination in faculty employment for which universities can be assigned the responsibility. A full analysis of the supply side should be a major element in any such calculation. The above material also indicates that numerical goals for a university's hiring of female and black faculty in particular fields, based on separate "pools" (by sex and race) of persons assumed to be qualified, can be significantly biased by incorrect estimates of qualified supply. That subject is treated in the next two chapters.

The data in this chapter show why a significant part of government affirmative action programs should be directed at improvement in the quality of supply of women and members of minorities for faculty appointments, especially in the upper reaches of the academic world. There can be no doubt that affirmative action efforts on the supply side are a necessary part of lasting improvement in the utilization of the talents of members of minorities and women as teacher-scholars in universities.

4. *Federal Guidelines for Faculty Employment*

This chapter and the next analyze the comprehensive federal scheme of regulation, developed under Executive orders and administrative rulings and designed to assure compliance by federal contractors (including universities holding research contracts) with the requirements in those orders and rulings. These two chapters will critically examine the labor market assumptions on which the enforcement requirements are based.

This chapter discusses the development by HEW of a set of guidelines for universities to follow in constructing and complying with their affirmative action plans and examines the special "availability-utilization" analysis that HEW requires universities to use to measure the extent of their alleged discrimination. Chapter 5 takes up various aspects of goal setting and goal enforcement and different kinds of affirmative action goals.

THE DEVELOPMENT OF HIGHER EDUCATION GUIDELINES

An indication at the outset of certain governmental features of the comprehensive scheme of regulation under Executive Order No. 11246 for federal contractors may help in understanding recent developments under the order and its application to universities.

As explained in Chapter 1, the contractor compliance scheme was developed in the Department of Labor, with HEW serving as the enforcement agency for universities and colleges. The scheme has been established and developed by Executive order, without Congressional consideration or endorsement. It is enforced exclusively by administrative-agency action. The penalty for noncompliance takes the form of withdrawal of part or all of the contractor's eligibility for federal contracts. Government regulation under Executive Order No. 11246 is separate from and in addition to, the fairly comprehensive, legislatively established programs for attacking employment discrimination discussed in Chapter 1.

As federal contractors, the major universities of this country, both public and private, are subject to Executive Order No. 11246 and to Executive Order No. 11375, which added "sex" to the protected categories. The faculties of the major universities (which include most of the top natural scientists, life scientists, social scientists, and humanities scholars in this country) and the positions they hold are subject to the rules and requirements of the applicable provisions of those Executive orders dealing with the employment, advancement, and compensation of workers.

Executive Order No. 11246 provides that all contractors must agree to abide by the following provision in all parts of their operations during the performance of such a contract:

(1) The contractor will not discriminate against any employee or applicant for employment because of race, color, religion, sex, or national origin. The contractor will take affirmative action to ensure that applicants are employed, and that employees are treated during employment, without regard to their race, color, religion, sex, or national origin.

Clearly, under that nondiscrimination clause, a university contractor must not discriminate either against or in favor of members of minority groups, women, or white males. There must be equal employment opportunity for each and every individual regardless of his or her race, color, religion, sex, or ethnic origin. Nevertheless, some provisions of the HEW Guidelines and some enforcement of the guidelines and regulations issued under Executive Order No. 11246 are not fully consistent with that provision.

Executive Order No. 11246 gives the Secretary of Labor the power to adopt rules, regulations, and orders as he deems necessary and appropriate to achieve the objectives of, and compliance with, that order. In that connection, the development of the notion of affirmative action under the Department of Labor's regulations is of interest. In the May 1968 regulation (Code of Federal Regulations, Title 41, Chapter 60-1), the kinds of affirmative actions specified were: to post the required statement of nondiscrimination in conspicuous places, to include it in all solicitations and advertisements for employees, and to notify any collective bargaining agent of the contractor's agreement not to discriminate. Provision was made for enforcement through the contractor furnishing information and reports and through investigation by the Department of Labor (or the appropriate federal agency designated by the Department of Labor) to ascertain compliance with the Executive order and with the rules, regulations, and relevant orders of the Secretary of Labor. If the investigation should reveal any lack of compliance (termed *deficiencies*), the contractor was (and still is) required to make a commitment to correct such deficiencies before the contractor can be found to be in compliance with the Executive order and, therefore, an eligible bidder on federal contracts.

On December 4, 1971, the Secretary of Labor added a whole new set of requirements for compliance. They provided that each federal contractor[1] in any line of activity must develop a written affirmative action program and must do so according to certain especially developed techniques. For determining deficiencies in the employment of women and minority-group members, the contractor must use a prescribed statistical method for calculating available and qualified supply for each job classification.[2] As we shall see, the method, though perhaps usable and appropriate for jobs requiring manual qualifications and skills, is inappropriate for quite individualized positions that require rare combinations of qualities, such as is the case for most tenure positions at major universities.

The contractor, using the prescribed statistical method, is required to calculate his deficiencies in numbers for women and members of minorities for each job classification, and to set forth specific hiring goals for women and members of minorities, in numerical terms and with hiring timetables attached to the numbers. Those numerical hiring goals, supposedly designed to remedy the calculated deficiencies, are not absolute commitments but are to be pursued by the contractor "applying every good faith effort to make all aspects of [his] affirmative action program work."

Strict adherence to proper rules and procedures to ensure that women and members of minorities are widely encouraged to apply for any job openings and are given equal opportunity for employment, training, promotion, and fair compensation no longer sufficed to meet compliance requirements. The additional concepts,

[1] Specifically, each contractor or subcontractor with a federal contract of $50,000 or more and 50 or more employees. Public institutions and agencies with federal contracts were required to have written affirmative action plans beginning October 4, 1972.

[2] Job classification "meaning one or a group of jobs having similar content, wage rates, and opportunities"—a vague and unsatisfactory definition.

method of determining and measuring discrimination, and other added requirements for compliance are embodied in a new Part 60-2 of Chapter 60 of Title 41 of the Code of Federal Regulations, commonly referred to as Revised Order No. 4.[3]

The methodological and goal requirements contained in Revised Order No. 4 were devised by the Department of Labor for more rapid and effective elimination of race discrimination in the building trades. The order spread that elaborate system to industry in general.

As the federal "administering agency" to enforce compliance by universities and colleges with the Executive orders and Revised Order No. 4, HEW had the task of making the rule modifications and adaptations necessary and desirable to fit the special characteristics and circumstances of the 900-odd institutions of higher education covered by those orders. In addition, the 10 regional offices were making inconsistent rulings and questionable interpretations in a way that caused great concern among universities. It had become clear by early 1972 that some written guidelines, rules, and interpretations of orders and regulations as applied to universities were badly needed.

After repeated delays, at the end of July 1972 a 100-page draft of guidelines for the application of the Executive orders and Revised Order No. 4 to institutions of higher education was prepared and sent to some two dozen university officials for their personal review and their comment by mid-August, as it was hoped that a guidelines document could be published by the opening of the academic year in September.

The 100-page draft was a most disturbing document. Written in a rather accusatory and involved manner, it added a set of new requirements not in any previous orders and rulings,[4] which would

[3] See *Federal Register* (1971*b*).

[4] For example, five pages were devoted to some 14 "principles" (really mostly practices) for the handling of employee complaints or grievances. Some of those principles were clearly unsound and inconsistent with accepted practice in industrial relations. Presented as a single set of conflict-resolution procedures to handle any complaint (whether related to proscribed discrimination in employment or not), they provided that every grievance should be heard by a committee containing representation of women and minority groups, that the grievant should have the right of access to any file he or she deemed necessary in connection with the complaint (presumably including the private files of faculty colleagues), that there should be a formal transcript or recording of the proceedings, and that the institution would be bound to accept whatever

have involved considerable HEW intrusion into the internal affairs of universities—into educational policy and internal administration as well as employment practices. It was quite evident that those in authority in HEW's Office for Civil Rights had insufficient understanding of, or experience in, the operation of universities.

Some of the university officials who had received the document presented to the appropriate officials in the Department of Labor their strong objections to parts of the HEW draft. The Director of Federal Contract Compliance in the Department of Labor has to approve any regulations, directives, or orders to be issued by a federal agency to which the Department of Labor has delegated compliance authority under Executive Order No. 11246 and Revised Order No. 4.[5]

The Department of Labor officials, recognizing that the 100-page draft was unnecessarily detailed, ambiguous, and intrusive, instructed HEW to develop a new draft cut down perhaps to one-third the size, tightly organized and objectively written. It was suggested that misconceptions such as were contained in the 100-page document could be avoided if HEW had available for consultation an advisory panel of persons well versed in the actual operations of institutions of higher education. This idea seemed to find some support in the Department of Labor but has not been used by HEW.

Without any further consultation with persons in the colleges or universities, HEW issued its guidelines in October 1972. For the most part, these guidelines follow the specifications stated by the Department of Labor. They are based on Revised Order No. 4, adopting, without much adaptation, its methodology and its scheme for determining numerical goals.

---

decision such a grievance committee might make but the grievant had no obligation whatsoever to accept a committee decision. Although there is presumably no obligation for an institution to adopt any such grievance procedures under the Executive orders or Revised Order No. 4, the draft stated that the absence of such a grievance procedure "may be viewed by the Office for Civil Rights in the context of a review or investigation as evidence of a contractor's intention not to act affirmatively to eliminate discrimination prohibited by the executive order."

[5] The pertinent provision in Chapter 60 of Title 41 of the Code of Federal Regulations [60-1.6(c)] reads as follows: "*Agency regulations.* The head of each agency shall prescribe regulations for the administration of the order and the regulations in his part. Agency regulations, directives and orders for such purpose must be submitted to the Director prior to issuance and may be enforced upon approval of the Director or 60 days after submission if not disapproved by the Director" (*Federal Register,* 1971*b*).

The final HEW Guidelines issued in October do embody some improvements. The procedures for notification and conduct of on-site compliance investigations, for noncompliance determinations, and for hearings are more reasonable, but difficult issues (such as federal agency access to and use of confidential letters of evaluation of faculty members by prominent scholars in the field) remain unresolved. Provision seems to be made in the following statement for numerical hiring goals on a broad enough basis for the statistical law of averages to have some application: "In many institutions the appropriate unit for goals is the school or division (e.g., of humanities departments, social science departments, natural science departments) rather than the department" (Office for Civil Rights, 1972, p. J5). However, some regional offices have been insisting on hiring goals by academic department almost as though that statement did not exist.

The guidelines do seem to recognize that preferential treatment in the selection of faculty according to race, sex, religion, or national origin constitutes discrimination in violation of Executive Order No. 11246. However, the issue is confused by an extreme, untypical example. The guidelines' wording is as follows:

> In the area of academic appointments, a nondiscriminatory selection process does not mean that an institution should indulge in "reverse discrimination" or "preferred treatment" which leads to the selection of unqualified persons over qualified ones. Indeed to take such action on grounds of race, ethnicity, sex or religion constitutes discrimination in violation of the Executive Order (ibid., p. 8).

Of course, the appropriate example would be the more typical case of the hiring of a less-qualified person over a better-qualified person on grounds of sex, race, or other group or class affiliation in order to meet numerical goals.

The HEW Guidelines do not attempt to reconcile the conflicting aims of nondiscrimination and equal employment opportunity on the one hand and insistence on hiring of substantially more women and members of minorities to achieve proportional representation according to numerical hiring goals on the other. That dilemma puts universities in a difficult position. Section 703(j) of Title VII of the Civil Rights Act of 1964, which has applied to institutions of higher education since March 24, 1972, reads as follows:

> Nothing contained in this title shall be interpreted to require an employer . . . to grant preferential treatment to any individual or to any group because of the race, color, religion, sex, or national origin of such individual or group on account of an imbalance which may exist with respect to the total number or percentage of persons of any race, color, religion, sex, or national origin employed by an employer . . . in comparison with the total number or percentage of such race, color, religion, sex, or national origin in any community, state, section, or other area, or in the available work force in any community, state, section, or other area.

Chief Justice Burger, speaking for the majority of the U.S. Supreme Court in *Griggs v. Duke Power* (1971) declared that under Title VII, "Discriminatory preference for any group, minority or majority, is precisely and only what Congress has proscribed." The Court went on to support individual merit as the basis for selection and reward, declaring: "Congress has not commanded that the less qualified be preferred over the better qualified simply because of minority origins. Far from disparaging job qualifications, Congress has made such qualifications the controlling factor, so that race, religion, nationality, and sex become irrelevant."

"AVAILABILITY ANALYSIS" FOR MEASURING DISCRIMINATION

The HEW Guidelines instruct universities and colleges how to determine whether women and minority persons are "underutilized," and therefore, discriminated against "in any job classification or organizational unit" (Office for Civil Rights, 1972, pp. J1 to J5). The guidelines assume that each academic rank (e.g., professor, associate professor, assistant professor) is a separate job classification.

Referring to the "required analysis" as "a unique aspect of equal employment opportunity under the Executive Order," the guidelines recognize that there are problems in applying the "analysis" to "academic personnel" because "the recruiting area will vary from institution to institution" and "may be a national or even international one," and because "the skills required for a particular position are often quite specialized" so that "accurate information on availability may be more difficult to obtain."

The guidelines state that "for academic employees the basic national data on earned doctoral degrees will provide the basis for a utilization analysis of the contractor's work force, unless the contractor can otherwise demonstrate that the labor market upon which it draws is significantly different from this base." With respect to tenured faculty, the guidelines state: "To determine the number of women available for senior positions, the Office [for Civil Rights of HEW] recommends that the contractor use data available from the National Register of Scientific and Technical Personnel prepared by the National Science Foundation, and the U.S. Office of Education's annual reports on earned degrees"—presumably Ph.D. degrees—for university positions.[6]

Each university must compare, "by comparable job categories," "the number of women and minorities in its current workforce" with their estimated availability according to "availability analysis." "Wherever the comparison reveals that a hiring unit of the university (a department or section) is not employing minorities and women to the extent that they are available and qualified for work, it is then required to set" numerical hiring goals to overcome any such "deficiencies in the utilization of minorities and women."

The availability-utilization analysis is obviously a kind of supply-demand analysis, which assumes that nondiscrimination will always result in a university employing women and members of minorities in each "job category" and each "hiring unit" in exact proportion to their representation in the supply that is qualified for the demand. Such a statistical technique should, therefore, be applied only after a thorough analysis of the various qualifications that supply must have for particular faculty positions and a similar thorough analysis of the requirements for the faculty positions—the demand. Otherwise, any disproportions between calculated "utilization" and actual "utilization" may just be mistakes in the numbers used and not evidence of discrimination for which the university is alone responsible and which nondiscrimination on the part of the university would eliminate.

From various statements in the guidelines, it is obvious that the HEW enforcement staff have not made any careful analysis of qualified supply for different faculty positions in different disci-

[6] In any year, probably the sex representation among the top 10 percent of Ph.D. recipients in the country is about the same as that for all other Ph.D. recipients that year. However, there certainly could be a difference between the proportion of women in the top 10 percent and in the other 90 percent of Ph.D. recipients in particular disciplines and subfields of disciplines (e.g., theoretical and applied branches of a subject). It would be extremely difficult and quite costly for each major university to try to determine whether such differences actually exist for each subfield and each discipline and to do so in terms of the qualifications for particular faculty positions at that institution. More on this subject anon.

plines. For example, repeatedly in the guidelines, the absence of women or members of minorities in an academic department is referred to as "exclusion" on the part of the institutions and as a "deficiency" (meaning discrimination by the institution), regardless of the amount of fully qualified supply of women or blacks actually available for each of the faculty positions in that discipline or department.

HEW avoids responsibility by requiring the universities themselves to make numerical estimates of their so-called deficiencies according to the prescribed technique, even though proper data may not be obtainable or the technique cannot properly be applied to some or all faculty positions in a particular department. However, if the university, using the technique with inadequate data, comes up with no deficiency or an exceedingly small one (a fraction of a person less than half),[7] the HEW compliance officials may refuse to approve the university's affirmative action plan on the grounds that the technique was not properly applied and that some specific hiring goals for such departments have to be included in the plan. The only appeal from such a decision presumably is higher up in the executive branch of the federal government. Persons in the federal government could hardly be sufficiently informed and expert to decide what the proper hiring goals at various faculty ranks in all disciplines in a particular university should be. Yet the staffs of HEW regional offices, who lack such expertise, negotiate with universities and approve or disapprove submitted affirmative action plans required to contain such goals. Under the circumstances, it is not surprising that they make a variety of "demands" on universities that go far beyond numerical goals.

THE INAPPROPRIATENESS OF "AVAILABILITY ANALYSIS"

From the analysis of supply and of demand for tenure positions in major universities set forth in Chapters 2 and 3, it is evident that the required "availability-utilization" technique cannot properly be applied to most tenure positions in such institutions. That tech-

[7] Such a result is likely in many disciplines, since blacks apparently hold no more than 1 percent of all Ph.D. degrees (Bryant, 1969) and since in particular disciplines women earned the following percentages of the Ph.D. degrees granted during the decade of the 1960s: engineering, 0.4 percent; physics, 2.0 percent; geology, 2.5 percent; business and commerce, 2.8 percent; religion in liberal arts, 4.5 percent; economics, 5.6 percent; mathematics, 6.5 percent; chemistry and statistics, 6.8 percent. The average size of academic departments in the arts and sciences at major private universities seems to be between 15 and 20 regular faculty.

nique, and the assumptions on which it is based, just will not provide proper answers about discrimination and proportional representation, given the facts of the situation. And to derive numerical goals by such a technique and to enforce compliance with them for the tenured faculty is almost bound to create some demand discrimination in faculty employment.

The reasons that the technique is so unsuitable for the situation can be briefly explained by drawing on the conclusions in Chapters 2 and 3.

Dealing first with the supply side, it has been explained that great variation exists in the mental and other personal qualities that are basic considerations in faculty appointment in major universities: (1) teaching ability at various levels and by various methods in particular specialties, (2) ability to produce important research contributions and to make teaching and research mutually reinforcing, and (3) ability to contribute constructively to the career development of colleagues and to the effective operation of one's department and the university (collegial and managerial contributions).

The requisite qualifications for appointment to tenure are likely to be possessed by fewer and fewer persons (1) the higher the level of excellence of a university and (2) the rarer the qualities (including training) necessary for advanced teaching and scholarship in the specialty. That explains why the number of qualified persons anywhere in the world for particular tenure appointments at a distinguished American university are generally very small.

On top of that, the supply configuration for married women, in contrast to that for men and single women, generally is a pyramid that falls off sharply at the upper levels of tenure positions for major universities. Presumably that configuration for married women should be taken into account in any availability-utilization analysis.

As was noted in Chapter 3, qualified supply for tenured faculty positions in universities usually is specified in terms of a subfield or a combination of two subfields of the discipline. In an economics department, for example, the subfields might include the following 13: microeconomic theory, macroeconomic theory, econometrics, economic development and growth, economic history, industrial organization and price policy, international economics, labor economics, mathematical economics, money and financial institutions, public finance, urban economics, and centrally planned economies.

An economics department might have 30 to 35 faculty (say, two-thirds with tenure) distributed among those 13 subfields. Even within subfields, there is further specialization. A faculty position in international economics might stress specialization in international-trade theory, or commercial policy, or international finance, or international investment and foreign aid. A faculty position in labor economics might stress labor markets including wage theory, labor relations including unions, or manpower training and development. For a tenure opening in international-trade theory, persons in the other three specialties in the subfield would not be likely to qualify. For an opening in labor economics stressing theory, specialists in labor relations or manpower would not be likely to qualify. Thus, a proper availability analysis would, in most instances, need to be made on the basis of specialties within subfields within departments.

Where the number of women or blacks considered qualified for tenure in a department of a major university is quite small and that small number is scattered among several subfields, the use of availability analysis becomes exceedingly dubious. For instance, faculty in top-ranked mathematics departments, in connection with developing affirmative action plans, have stated that no more than one or possibly two female mathematicians in this country could at this time, on the basis of scholarly qualifications, be offered a tenure post in one of the top dozen mathematics departments. Similarly, in trying to apply availability analysis, the number of female economists considered by faculty in leading departments to be qualified for appointment to a tenure opening in one of the top dozen economics departments has been variously given as between 9 and 12, distributed among more than half a dozen subfields. Corresponding figures for blacks would apparently be none in mathematics and 4 or 5 in economics.[8]

With such small numbers and with tenure positions coming open on the average perhaps every 15 or 20 years (turnover of tenured faculty recently seems to have been averaging around 3 or 4 percent), the purpose to be served by requiring each economics department in major universities now to apply the required "availability" analysis and come up with numerical goals for women and black economists by department, making allowance for subfields, is

[8] In view of the numbers of nontenured female faculty, particularly in economics, these numbers can be expected to increase somewhat over the next five years.

unclear—unless it is to stimulate bidding for the female and black economists, several of whom have had all kinds of offers and do not seem to be movable. It is even more questionable to require the top mathematics departments to engage in the required analysis and to set numerical hiring goals for women and blacks for any tenure opening that may occur in one of a number of subfields as a result of death, retirement, or interinstitutional movement of faculty.

Under such circumstances, the prescribed "availability" analysis clearly does not measure discrimination in demand by a particular department. It is difficult to know just what it would measure.

To make a somewhat meaningful estimate of the qualified, available supply for all tenure positions at major institutions is a difficult task, even assuming a significant range for error. The academic departments in the arts and sciences at major institutions may average around 35 in number. The number of subfields per department may average 7 or 8.[9] Disregarding the need in many cases to take account of specialties in subfields, that could mean some 700 to 800 estimates ($35 \times 7 \times 3$—one for total number and one each for women and members of minorities, in the subfield). That quantity of estimates would be required, say, for 400 tenure positions in a total full-time faculty of perhaps 650. Separate estimates for tenured and nontenured faculty would seem necessary and would double the number of estimates in each case. Persons qualified for a nontenure appointment generally would not be qualified for a tenure appointment.

In addition to the large numbers of estimates needed and the conceptual problems, there is another complication. "Minorities" is an ambiguous, quite heterogeneous category consisting of "Negroes, Spanish-surnamed, American Indians, and Orientals." "Spanish-surnamed" includes Puerto Ricans, Cubans, Mexican-Americans, and descendants of Spanish immigrants—how far back and in what ratio of Spanish blood is unclear. Orientals are well represented in tenure positions in major universities, not only in positions in Chinese and Japanese art, literature, history, and politics but also in the distinguished mathematics, physics, economics, and engineering departments. Separate estimates presumably should be made, at least for some of the constituent minority

[9] History has perhaps the most subfields of any discipline with at least three types of limiting criteria for each position: (1) country or geographic area, (2) chronological period, and (3) special subject matter—diplomatic, political, cultural, intellectual, art, economic, urban, etc.

groups; a single estimate for all of them combined may have little meaning for the question of discrimination.

Although availability analysis may be inappropriate and biasing for tenured faculty, it can have some validity and usefulness for application to the large numbers finishing their Ph.D. requirements and seeking term appointments as assistant professor or instructor. In a sense there is a labor market for the new Ph.D. recipients who seek appointment each year to instructorships and assistant professorships. In this country, some 18,000 to 20,000 Ph.D. degrees are earned annually by graduate students in the sciences, the social sciences, and the humanities. As explained in Chapter 2, most of them seek academic appointments early in the calendar year in which they plan to complete their Ph.D. training. A relatively high turnover in instructorships and assistant professorships is characteristic of major universities. On the average probably 15 to 20 percent of their assistant professorships become open each year compared with a figure of around 3 or 4 percent for tenure positions.

The supply of new Ph.D.'s coming on the market each year is, of course, differentiated in many important respects. They include intellectual capacity, quality of graduate training, field and subfield of study, probable abilities in teaching, potential for significant research, gifts for academic administration, etc. Nevertheless, one would expect that at that point in career development, there would be no significant sex differential in ability and potential as teacher-scholars. In other words, one would assume that the top 10 percent in qualifications (appropriately measured) should be distributed by sex in about the same ratio as the next 25 percent of all new Ph.D.'s. The same sex ratio might not hold, however, for (say) the top 10 percent in a discipline, particularly one in which women earn relatively few Ph.D.'s, such as astrophysics, economics, various branches of engineering, geology, mathematics, and physics. On the other hand, the proportion of women in the top 10 percent of the new Ph.D.'s in English and certain foreign languages and literatures might be relatively high. Also, one could expect some deviation from the overall sex ratio in certain subfields, partly perhaps in terms of their degree of abstraction. Indeed, although differentiation by subfield is generally not very far along at the time of Ph.D. completion, such differentiation can make the assumption of normal sex distribution of talent and training for individual subfields very questionable. The case for stating a numerical hiring goal for, say, three similar disciplines combined instead of one, rests in good part on the likelihood of unusual supply conditions with respect to some particular openings.

Despite such problems, material presented above shows that differentiation and specialization on the supply side are much greater five or seven years after receipt of the Ph.D. degree. For that reason, properly based, numerical hiring goals for faculty of major institutions are more appropriate at the new Ph.D. level than they are at a later stage in faculty careers.

The characteristics of demand for faculty at the new Ph.D. stage are likely to fit with the supply characteristics in a higher percentage of cases than is true at later career stages. Partly that is because there is apt to be less differentiation on both sides of the market at the new assistant professor stage. The demand for new assistant professors is likely to involve considerable teaching in elementary courses and over a wider range of subfields, since the candidates will have just completed their graduate training and recently taken their general examinations. The demand by academic institutions is, of course, also concentrated heavily in the early months of the calendar year, and the numbers of candidates considered fully qualified for assistant professorships in major universities is generally much larger than is true for tenure openings.

Consideration of the difficulties with the prescribed availability analysis and analysis of supply-and-demand conditions in this chapter provide a basis for examination of government-required hiring goals for university faculty—the subject of the next chapter.

5. *Affirmative Action Goals for Faculty*

The federal government's current program to eliminate bias in university employment through federal contract regulation rests mainly on numerical hiring goals[1] and schedules ("timetables") for fulfillment of the goals. As applied to major universities, the scheme of goal requirements raises such troublesome questions as the following:

1 What notions concerning the causes and cures for race and sex bias in faculty employment underlie HEW's scheme of numerical goals with timetables?

2 To what extent is "proportional representation" by sex, race, or religion a soundly conceived goal for faculty employment, both tenure and nontenure?

3 To what extent will numerical goals derived by the prescribed method and negotiated with HEW lead to inflated goals that can only be met by giving some women and minority-group members preference in hiring, promotion, and/or salary?

4 What provisions are there in the present HEW scheme to determine whether the numerical goals universities have actually set are too high in some disciplines for some ranks?

5 To what extent will inflated goals and pressures for their achievement create new, additional discrimination and tend to develop a two-standard faculty?

[1] They really are hiring and promotion goals, since HEW has, in some cases, not only asked universities for the number of hires but also required that the goals include "the projected overall composition of the faculty in the unit"—in other words, the sex and race composition of the department one, two, three, or more years hence by rank.

6 What are the effects of numerical hiring and promotion goals on the integrity of departmental and university arrangements for determining appointment, promotion, and salary on the basis of merit?

7 If a particular academic department should fail to meet its numerical hiring goal, should sanctions be imposed on the department and its individual members, or would such sanctions be unjust and violate individuals' academic rights and academic freedom?

8 What attention and weight should be given to other goals such as improving the quality of supply or achieving "diversity" in the faculty?

Those questions will be taken up in order, after a brief look at directive statements concerning numerical goals and timetables in Revised Order No. 4, which is the basic document.

Federal contractors covered by that order are required to conduct "availability analyses" both to measure disproportionality (that is, discrimination on the demand side) and to determine the precise numbers, as goals for hiring, that a contractor must adopt. To quote again from the order:

> An acceptable affirmative action program must include an analysis of areas within which the contractor is deficient in the utilization of minority groups and women, and further, goals and timetables to which the contractor's good faith efforts must be directed to correct the deficiencies and thus to increase materially the utilization of minorities and women, at all levels and in all segments of his work force where deficiencies exist.

It is further stated that "goals should be specific for planned results, with timetables for completion," and "must be targets reasonably attainable by means of applying every good faith effort to make all aspects of the entire affirmative action program work."

Those statements contain four significant facts about the mandatory numerical goals in affirmative action plans. One, such goals are based entirely on availability analysis and, therefore, raise all the questions that such analysis raises and are invalid to the extent that that analysis is invalid. Two, numerical goals take the supply side as given and assume that the demand side is responsible for any "deficiencies" (discrimination) and that the demand side must, therefore, take the affirmative actions through the hiring and promotion of members of minorities and women. Three, numerical goals assume that proportional representation, as measured by availability analysis, is the norm for all sections of university faculties and that proportional representation for women and minority groups would exist throughout a faculty if there were no discrimination on the demand side. Four, the goal setting and timetables are in terms of actual hires; they are result-oriented instead of process-oriented, with no account taken by the enforcement agency (HEW for higher education) of their discrimination-creating potential. Specifically, all the pressures and incentives are directed toward achieving a particular number of women and members of minorities among the new hires.

BASIS FOR HEW-PRESCRIBED GOALS

In placing primary emphasis on goal making by colleges and universities, the HEW Guidelines assume that most of the responsibility for race or sex bias in faculties of universities and colleges rests on the demand side. The primacy of goal making and goal enforcement also assumes that race and sex bias in faculties can be largely overcome through government pressures to achieve certain quantities of appointments and promotions for women and blacks and members of other minorities.

As material already presented has indicated, those assumptions are not well founded. In many disciplines of the arts and sciences, serious deficiencies exist on the supply side, especially for positions in the upper faculty ranks in major universities. The need for a significant supply component in a federal antibias program has already been explained, so it is not necessary to belabor the matter here. Chapter 9 contains a specific proposal for post-Ph.D. training while on regular faculty appointment that would significantly increase the number of women and members of minorities qualified for tenure appointments in major universities in fields where they are now quite scarce.

Further attention, however, needs to be given to such matters as (1) the proper base for proportionality calculations for goal purposes and (2) the validity of applying proportionality with timetables to certain faculty positions.

With respect to faculty in major institutions, what is the base or unit of "qualified" supply from which to establish a numerical goal? Under the HEW Guidelines, a hiring goal is to be determined by the difference between the proportion of each race, sex, etc., in the total qualified supply available to the university for appointment in the unit and the proportion actually employed in that unit by the university.

The proper unit for goal making and goal enforcement, thus, is a crucial matter. Should all numerical goals be calculated and enforced by a unit that is defined as the faculty of the arts and sciences college as a whole, a division of that college (for example, physical sciences, social sciences, humanities), each academic department, each subfield of a discipline, each faculty rank in the units just mentioned, or a particular opening (for example, a position in medieval history, modern Chinese politics, or public finance)?

On the appropriate unit for goal making and goal enforcement, the HEW Guidelines are equivocal and unenlightening. The wording is as follows:

> In many institutions the appropriate unit for goals is the school or division, rather than the department. While estimates of availability in academic employment can best be determined on a disciplinary basis, anticipated turnover and vacancies can usually be calculated on a wider basis. While a school, division or college may be the organizational unit which assumes responsibility for setting and achieving goals, departments which have traditionally excluded women or minorities from their ranks are expected to make particular efforts to recruit, hire and promote women and minorities. In other words, the Office for Civil Rights will be concerned not only with whether a school meets its overall goals, but also whether apparent general success has been achieved only by strenuous efforts on the part of a few departments (Office for Civil Rights, 1972, p. J5).

Note that the absence of women from a department's "ranks" is assumed to be a result of the department's "traditional exclusion" on the demand side and that "success" is assumed to be directly related to the "strenuousness" of the university's efforts.

Certainly the most appropriate unit would be one in which the supply—overall and by sex and by race—was sufficiently homogeneous to warrant the application of the principle of proportionality as a norm. For most tenure positions in major universities, such a supply situation does not exist. It is on those grounds that the calculation of numerical goals for tenured faculty of major universities and their enforcement by HEW is considered unwarranted and misleading.

As explained in Chapter 4, the serious objections to the HEW method can be partly met if the composition of the unit for goal making is confined to persons seeking their first regular faculty appointment as assistant professor at the end of their Ph.D. training, and if the unit is broad enough to include three or more departments so that there are sufficient openings each year and a sufficient supply in total and by sex or race for the combined openings. At the point of Ph.D. completion, the supply has a considerable amount of common, up-to-date training. The demand is likely, even at that stage, to be differentiated to a significant extent by subfield or subfields, though much less so than at a later stage in career development. However, with a sufficiently large unit, those subfield differences would tend to average out. It is assumed that, for such a unit, the distribution of supply of women, and perhaps blacks, according to qualifications for appointment might have much the same configuration as for white males.

On that basis, numerical goals might be calculated and projected by sex and race within a range of probability for first post-Ph.D. appointment as assistant professor. A proposal to that effect is set forth in some detail in Chapter 9.

INFLATED GOALS AND THEIR CONSEQUENCES

The HEW method, particularly if applied by academic departments to tenure positions in major universities, is likely to lead to inflated goals. That is so for several reasons. One, the assumption that the demand side is responsible for any disproportionality and that such disproportionality must be corrected through hiring enough women and members of minorities in itself tends to lead to inflated numerical goals. It inflates the responsibility of the demand side. Two, both HEW and the universities, in the absence of proper supply figures for each institution for each departmental subfield in which a vacancy is predicted, use the total of Ph.D. holders in the discipline or the Ph.D. recipients during a past period, say 5 to 15 years before. Such figures tend to inflate the numbers for women and blacks because they do not take account of the amount and quality of developmental experience during the first five to seven years as assistant professor. Three, in many cases, the numbers of tenured faculty in a department are so small that the proportionate figure for women (or "underrepresented" minority groups combined) is only a fraction—frequently well under one-half. The tendency is to round the figure to one if only to avoid the misinterpretation that the department considers no woman or minority person qualified for any tenure openings in that department in the near future.[2] Four, several universities may independently assume that each of them will be able to attract one out of (say) a dozen women in the country qualified for tenure appointment. If all three to four dozen major universities project as a goal one woman on tenure in that department, the resulting goals taken together are inflated. Assuming that each of 36 major universities has a numerical goal of one female professor with tenure in a particular discipline and that 12 of the 36 have a female professor in that department, then the other 24 should seek to fulfill their goal of one by making a tenure offer to a woman at least by the time their timetable indicates. In other words, the potential demand for female professors in those major institutions has been tripled by the goal-setting process. As the 24 institutions make offers designed to attract some or all of the 12 women away from their existing positions, such actions will bid up these women's salaries above those for comparable males. A dual market will tend to develop—one for females and one for males. However, only 12 of the 36 universities will have a female tenured faculty member in that discipline after all the bidding has taken place. The other 24 will continue to have a "deficiency" as long as the supply of qualified women is not increased sufficiently or until they decide to lower standards in order to appoint a woman.[3] Acceleration of the timing of offers through unduly fast timetables—even too fast for appropriate openings to develop— serves, of course, as an additional demand-inflating factor. In some negotiations with universities, HEW field staff seem to be operating on the basis of the naïve statement in the HEW Guidelines that "in many cases" full accomplishment of numerical goals "within 5 years" would be "a reasonable

[2] This goal-inflation factor is undoubtedly one reason that HEW presses for numerical goals by department and is reluctant to accept a zero goal for a department even though the calculated figure for blacks and women is actually only a small fraction of one person. It is apparently on such grounds that MIT's affirmative action plan contains the statement that as of April 1973 "women and minorities are underrepresented in most academic positions within the Institute, particularly in faculty positions, both tenured and untenured" (see *Tech Talk,* 1973*a*).

[3] A university could hire a female assistant professor in hopes of developing her into a qualified professor with tenure or possibly bid such an assistant professor away from another institution that had a female assistant professor who was about qualified for a tenure appointment.

time" and that in other cases "more time or less time will be required" (Office for Civil Rights, 1972, p. J4).

HEW assumes no responsibility for any inflation in numerical goals, even though it may reject proposed affirmative action plans on the grounds that some of the numerical goals are not large enough or the timetables for their accomplishment are too extended. Also, HEW does not have a reporting system or statistical analyses designed to evaluate the extent to which the numerical goals of covered universities, or a category of institutions such as major universities, are inflated.

The smaller the unit for goal setting, the more necessary it becomes to predict the sex or race of individual appointments and promotions within that unit. Expectations and presumptions become attached to particular positions, and pressures, both internal and external (for example, by HEW and advocacy groups), are focused in a very specific, concrete manner. Thus, particular numerical goals exert a coercive influence.

The combination of inflated goals and strong pressures for their achievement have serious implications for a faculty system of appointment, promotion, and salary based on professional qualifications and performance. Selection of female and minority-group faculty members partly on grounds of sex or race is likely to create additional discrimination and can have quite undesirable effects on the utilization of the teaching and research resources of a university. Numerical goals that assume the promotion of particular female or minority-group assistant professors to tenure can be especially injurious over an extended period because they imply some disregard of open competition under merit-based systems for the determination of tenure appointments.

Significant deviations from choice of the best available person for a tenure position as judged by mature teacher-scholars under proper procedures is likely to cause faculty members, both tenured and nontenured, to lose confidence in the integrity of the system of professional determination of promotions and appointments to tenure. The number and ratio of "mistakes" that develop over time would increase, with adverse consequences described in Chapter 2. A two-status faculty would tend to develop: those who were chosen because their qualifications were judged by their professional peers to be the best for a position in open competition and those whose appointment occurred, in part, because of their physical characteristics—race or sex. The latter would begin to be considered as special EEO appointments and, if their effectiveness as teacher-scholars turned out to be comparatively low, they would be thought of as EEO "mistakes."

Such a situation could be embarrassing to all concerned. The opinions of colleagues and students would become evident in course elections and teaching assignments. The costs to the institution would take various forms, including faculty discontent, reduced faculty effectiveness, and less drawing power for able students and able faculty. Sex-conscious and race-conscious favoritism could also expose the university to charges of discrimination against the most able white, male applicants or assistant professors.

THE QUESTION OF SANCTIONS

Revised Order No. 4 states: "Supervisors should be made to understand that their work performance is being evaluated on the basis of their equal employment opportunity efforts and results, as well as other criteria" [par. 60-2.22(b) (8)]. Applying that idea to university faculty, it has been proposed that universities institute a system of sanctions to ensure compliance with affirmative action goals (Weitzman, 1973, pp. 500–501). Among the sanctions on a department and its individual members suggested by Professor Lenore J. Weitzman is the denial of salary increases to members of those departments that have not met affirmative action goals. Weitzman also suggests "linking" the following to "affirmative action progress:" the size of the departmental budget, the amount of university research funds granted to the department, university approval of members' applications for outside research grants, and travel allowances to professional meetings.

Such individual and collective sanctions would clearly involve attempting to coerce individual faculty in their judgments concerning the best-qualified persons for faculty appointments. Such coercion would threaten academic freedom. It would be destructive of systems of faculty appointment according to qualifications and salary increases based on performance. Such individual sanctions applied in a collective manner would be unjust to individual nontenured and tenured faculty members. Some of those selective sanctions, such as denial of salary increases, nonapproval of research applications, and selective restrictions on travel funds, would violate the tenure rights of professors in the penalized departments. The suggestion of such sanctions shows the dangers of overemphasis on the achievement of numerical hiring and promotion goals, even assuming that the goals were appropriate and were properly determined.

The federal government had not, at the time of writing, applied the sanction of partial or complete block on the flow of research funds to an institution because it had failed to achieve one or more of its numerical goals. The likelihood that such failure could be explained has meant that some university administrators are not as concerned as they should be if some of their numerical goals seem unrealistically high.

OTHER AFFIRMATIVE ACTION GOALS

As already explained, the most serious defect in the HEW program of affirmative action goals for university faculty is the absence of goals for the supply side. Such goals should be formulated primarily in terms of training and development—both Ph.D. training and on-the-job development to qualify for a position with tenure, particularly at major institutions.

Such a program for improving the supply of highly qualified female and minority-group teacher-scholars in selected disciplines is presented in detail in the appendix to Chapter 9. Under the program, universities would submit affirmative action supply plans that would aim at certain numbers of women and blacks to be trained in a Ph.D. program in a discipline or to receive further on-the-job development in a discipline while serving as full-time or part-time assistant professors. The federal government would select from among the plans offered, certain university plans, either Ph.D. or postdoctoral, for approval. The approved plans would become part of a university's overall affirmative action program.

The purpose of the affirmative action supply program would be to attract and train a sufficient number of women and blacks in teaching and scholarship so that the discipline would have a critical mass of leading teacher-scholars with excellent doctoral and postdoctoral training. The present affirmative action plans specify only the numerical composition of demand. In disciplines where the number of women and blacks with Ph.D. degrees is quite small, they tend to spread the female and minority-group faculty around, with perhaps only one in each department. Such separation may seem to be "tokenism" and may have the psychological disadvantages of "singleness."

Sex and race discrimination in university faculties have various psychological aspects. Career aspirations and expectancies are affected by colleagues' attitudes, students' attitudes, social pressures and slights. Undoubtedly, wider and deeper understanding among male white faculty of the problems of a woman or a minority person on the faculty aids in progress toward the elimination of conscious and unconscious sex and race prejudices. However, it is difficult to conceive of specific goals or targets that could be developed and used for compliance purposes.

A number of groups have proposed diversity in the faculty as a hiring objective for colleges and universities. Unfortunately, the proposers are generally vague about the kinds of diversity they have in mind. And one cannot be sure whether "diversity" is proposed as an additional goal, as a substitute for numerical hiring goals aimed at proportional representation, or as part of those goals.

Diversity is stressed as a general kind of goal and is discussed from various angles in the 1973 report of the Committee on Discrimination of the American Association of University Professors ("Affirmative Action in Higher Education," 1973). The report begins with the statement that affirmative action must be "devised wholly consistent with the highest aspirations of universities and colleges for excellence and outstanding quality and that affirmative action should in no way use the very instrument of racial or sexual discrimination which it deplores." The committee then inconsistently commends "plans in which 'preference' and 'compensation' are words of positive connotation." "Compensation" is "for past failures to reach the actual market of intellectual resources available to higher education."[4] "Preference" seems to mean "affirmative consideration of race or sex," and preference to achieve "diversity" appears to the committee "to state a neutral, principled, and altogether precedented policy of preference" (ibid., p. 181). What the committee has in mind, however, is not clear from those statements.

As discussion of this subject in Chapter 2 indicates, diversity in university faculties has many dimensions besides race and sex. Particular kinds of diversity serve particular educational purposes. Consequently, it is necessary to think in terms of the kind of diversity necessary for particular departments and institutions and to recognize the need for balance among various values and objectives.

Unfortunately, the committee does not explain what diversity

[4] "Affirmative Action in Higher Education" (1973, p. 178). To an economist "failure to reach an actual market" might seem to imply deficiency on the supply side—failure to apply for a job—but it is evident in subsequent remarks that a deficiency in demand is assumed.

as a goal would mean in operational terms—how it should be defined, balanced against other values, and, particularly, how much weight should be given to diversity in selecting tenured or nontenured faculty compared with the stress put on the regular criteria of teaching, scholarship, and other contributions to the well-being of a university. Also there is the question whether the same kind of diversity is to be the goal in all departments in a uniform pattern. For enforcement by HEW compliance officers, some definite answers would need to be at hand.

The committee also proposes that a university "deliberately reserve discretion to depart from standards and criteria" generally applied in the selection and promotion of faculty, presumably including for tenure positions. It recommends that such "experimentation" be part of "the standard of a department or institution" in order to "help broaden the design of [an affirmative action] plan" (ibid., p. 178). However, the committee does not explain how an institution, following its advice, convinces a compliance officer that no sex discrimination has occurred when, as an experiment, a white male is appointed because, say, he seemed the best representative of the views of the radical left, or the radical right, or some particular religious or ethnic group. It is no answer to such problems to say, as the committee report does, that "at the present moment, the politics of reaction are a greater source for concern than the possibility that affirmative action might lend itself to heavy-handed bureaucratic misapplication" (ibid., p. 178).

The nation's leading universities have much to contribute to the solution of the problems of race, sex, and religious prejudice in career development and worklife in this country. Unwittingly to insist that they conform to a single design for affirmative action plans and goals, developed for industries like building construction and steel, is heavy-handed bureaucratic regulation. As the preceding pages have indicated and the chapters that follow further explain, HEW regulation of universities does have serious implications for their future progress.

STATEMENTS OF THE CARNEGIE COMMISSION

Chapters 1 through 5 of this study were in first draft in September 1973, before the Carnegie Commission's "Report and Recommendations" contained in *Opportunities for Women in Higher Education* was issued. On the basis of the material presented in the first five chapters, the author would question the wisdom of the following Commission recommendation concerning an affirmative action goal and timetable for each academic department:

2. Every department and school in an academic institution should establish, in consultation with the administration of the college or university, a goal relating to the relative representation of women on its regular faculty (assistant professor to full professor). In determining these goals, every appropriate source of information on the relative size of available pools of qualified women and men should be consulted—not just those indicated in the federal guidelines. A reasonable timetable for achieving the goals should be developed, but allowance should be made for special difficulties that may be encountered in adhering to the timetable, especially in fields in which there are currently relatively few women with doctor's degrees and in which competition among institutions for this limited pool of talent is likely to be intense (Carnegie Commission, 1973*b,* p. 148).

Questions can also be raised concerning the validity of the following statement:

The Commission believes that the evidence we have presented in Section 7 relating to the representation of women on college and university faculties, and to the lower salaries women receive, indicates clearly that a serious problem of discrimination exists and that the problem is particularly acute in the leading research universities and in the departments in those universities that have traditionally had predominantly male faculties (Carnegie Commission, 1973*b,* pp. 136–137).

The evidence referred to is in large measure the Scott study discussed toward the end of Chapter 3. That the problem of sex discrimination in salaries is "particularly acute" in the academic departments of major universities that have "predominantly male faculties" is doubtful. The material presented in Chapter 3 would indicate that if all factors are taken into account, especially on the supply side, the reverse is probably the case. Sex discrimination in salary, properly calculated, is probably less prevalent and less significant in the teaching faculties in arts and sciences in major universities than in other universities and colleges as a group.

6. *Faculty Cases under Federal and State Laws*

The differences in aim and legal basis between the HEW Guidelines and equal employment opportunity legislation come into focus in individual complaint cases. The federal Civil Rights Act of 1964 and the state fair employment practices laws[1] provide equal protection for all—males and females, black and white—based on qualifications. The HEW Guidelines, requiring specific, result-oriented hiring goals and timetables by sex and race, stimulate discrimination in favor of women and members of minorities. That is especially true where numerical goals are inflated.[2]

Generally speaking, preferential hiring for members of a particular race or sex, if practiced in individual cases, is likely to be in violation of the Civil Rights Act of 1964 and most of the state fair employment practices laws. Also, statistics can be used to support a complaint that a woman or a minority person was given preferential treatment in hiring or in promotion just as they have been used to support charges of discrimination against women and minority groups. For example, an affirmative action plan of a Midwestern university's politics department contains numerical goals as follows: a net increase in three years of 1 faculty member to a total of 49, to be achieved by decreasing the male faculty by 8 and

[1] Thirty-seven states have fair employment practices laws, but not all of those laws cover both public and private institutions of higher education. Also some cities, including Cleveland, New York, Philadelphia, Pittsburgh, and St. Louis, have municipal fair employment practices laws.

[2] Some writers contend that, under American constitutional law, there are serious doubts whether government-required, affirmative action hiring programs, which are "result-oriented" and aim at racial or sex balance in terms of specific numbers, are constitutional under the conditions in most universities. That is because they involve using race and sex as a criterion for employment and result in restricting the employment opportunities of "nonminority" individuals because of their race or sex. See Sherain (1973) and Bickel (1973, no. 73–235).

increasing the minority-group and female faculty from 6 to 15. In the New York State University system between the fall of 1970 and the fall of 1971, the total number of faculty increased from 9,492 to 9,608, or by 116. Of that increase of 116 faculty members, 111 were reported as "identified" with a minority group including women (Office of Equal Employment Opportunity Programs, 1972, p. 13). It might be difficult to explain how those results could be obtained without preferential hiring. Indeed, there is evidence that during that period women and members of minorities were given preference for appointment to certain faculty positions at the State University of New York at Albany and at other locations, in order to achieve affirmative action goals.[3]

CORRECTION OF BIAS

Extending back for decades, in many institutions of higher education, female faculty have been discriminated against by receiving less than equal pay[4] and having less than equal opportunity to advance in rank. Individuals have been handicapped in their career development by such discrimination in ways that often cannot, years later, be fully corrected.

In the case of female and minority-group faculty, the appropriate remedy would seem to be one aimed at correcting the situation insofar as that is possible for the particular faculty member or class of faculty members directly affected by discrimination. That is the aim and method of the Equal Employment Opportunity Commission, the state fair employment practices agencies, and the Equal Pay Division of the Department of Labor in enforcing the law against discrimination involving race, sex, color, or national origin. Indi-

[3] See Statement of the Anti-Defamation League of B'nai B'rith, submitted to the New York State Advisory Committee to the U.S. Commission on Civil Rights for inclusion in the Hearings in Albany on June 6 and 7, 1973, dealing with problems concerning Equal Employment Opportunity within the State University of New York.

[4] Equal pay for women for the performance of equal work is provided in the Fair Labor Standards Act administered by the Wage-Hour Division of the U.S. Department of Labor (university faculty have been covered since mid-1972) and in equal pay laws in 34 states, many of which have coverage that includes universities. The Fair Labor Standards Act also requires equal pay for men by forbidding employers to discriminate between male and female employees by paying lower wages or salaries to employees of one sex than to those of the other sex for equal work performed under similar working conditions that require equal skill, effort, and responsibility. The equal-pay provisions of the Fair Labor Standards Act apply only to discrimination based on sex and require that the lower rates of pay for one sex be raised to the higher rates for the other sex where a differential is established to be discriminatory.

vidual complaints are filed with those agencies, which investigate the complaints, and if there are reasonable grounds to believe that discrimination has occurred, prosecute the cases for the complainants, if necessary in court, and seek to achieve proper compensation and academic status. Corrective action may involve requiring a university to carry out some specific affirmative action program directed to the complaint in question.

By contrast, the HEW requirements for affirmative action programs are not designed to remedy specific discrimination against individuals. Rather, they aim to increase the hiring of women and blacks and members of other minorities in universities, whether those women and minority-group members have themselves ever been discriminated against in connection with university employment or not.

INCREASING NUMBER OF FORMAL COMPLAINTS

The number of complaints filed by faculty alleging discrimination in connection with their employment has been increasing and is expected to grow significantly in volume over the next two or three years. Some women's groups have recently been promoting the use of the courts. The 1972 amendments to the Civil Rights Act of 1964 extended its nondiscrimination provisions to all institutions of higher education and strengthened the powers of the Equal Employment Opportunity Commission (EEOC) to enforce Title VII of the act.

The total number of faculty complaints of discrimination filed with the government agencies and the courts at any one time is not known. There is no central reporting of all job discrimination complaints filed against colleges and universities with the Office for Civil Rights of HEW, the federal Equal Employment Opportunity Commission, the Department of Labor under the Equal Pay Act, the state and city agencies enforcing fair employment practices laws, and with the state and federal courts. Often the same complaint is filed with a number of agencies; a complaint may get settled at various points in the procedure; and complaints against higher education institutions are generally not separated into faculty and nonfaculty categories.

A basic reason for increasing faculty complaints of job bias is inconsistency in the federal programs themselves. As previously explained, the HEW Guidelines stimulate discrimination in favor of women and minority groups. They do so through alleging deficiencies that, in some cases, are not due to discrimination on the demand side, but must, the compliance officers insist, be corrected by the institution stating numerical hiring goals and using "good-faith efforts" to meet those goals.

On the other hand, the Civil Rights Act of 1964 clearly states that it is an unlawful employment practice to discriminate because of an individual's race, color, religion, sex, or national origin. Much the same language is in the state fair-practices acts. They provide that each job applicant must be treated as an individual, without regard to sex or race, and that employment or pay cannot be based on race, sex, or religion. The institutions of higher education are in the middle of a conflict between the guidelines as applied and enforced by HEW and the Civil Rights Act as interpreted by the U.S. Supreme Court.

Another reason for an increase in the number of complaints filed with the federal and state agencies is that those agencies often pay little or no attention to the existence and use of established faculty procedures for the settlement of charges of discrimination. The HEW Guidelines urge that universities have procedures for the fair handling of grievances as part of their affirmative action plans, but federal and state agencies handling individual complaints have often disregarded a complainant's failure or refusal to use the university's faculty grievance procedure before filing a complaint. Moreover, the government agency takes up a person's complaint free of charge and can seek to have the courts require that a university, if found in violation, increase the complainant's pay, compensate for past insufficiency through back pay, reappoint the complainant, appoint him or her if discrimination occurred in the appointment of someone else, and promote an assistant professor to tenure. Also, the federal or state agency has power to acquire data and access to confidential files and to hold open hearings or prosecute a case, if necessary, through the courts, on behalf of a complainant.

The HEW Office for Civil Rights assumes no responsibility if a university, following the instructions of an HEW compliance officer, is for that reason charged by EEOC, or a state agency, or a court, with discrimination against a white male applicant by hiring a less-qualified woman or black. In other words, a university can be charged at the same time with discrimination against women and blacks (by HEW because it has alleged "deficiencies" that must be "corrected" or by the EEOC or a state agency in individual cases of alleged past discrimination) and with discrimination against nonminority males (because the university favored women or blacks in hiring, which was the only way it could fulfill its affirmative action goals and meet timetables established according to instructions by HEW regional civil rights officials).

By October 1973, EEOC had some 600[5] individual complaints filed against colleges and universities, and HEW had received about 150 individual complaints of discrimination against nonminority males (in favor of women or blacks) or against women (in favor of blacks) in colleges and universities. It was not known against how many individual institutions complaints had been filed in both categories—discrimination against women and blacks and against nonminority whites. Since EEOC had a backlog of some 80,000 charges of employment discrimination, with 50,000 being filed each year, considerable delay in the handling of such complaints was to be expected.

The growing scarcity of faculty openings (with 100 to 500 applicants responding to an advertisement for an assistant professor opening in many disciplines) serves to enlarge the number of complaints of bias filed with government agencies or with the courts.

Under such conditions, failure to obtain a desirable faculty position for which one applied or into which one hoped to be promoted can prove to be quite a loss to the individual. Correspondingly, gaining a three-year appointment or a promotion to continuous tenure by filing a complaint followed by government action, can be quite valuable for the complainant.[6]

RESORT TO GOVERNMENT AGENCIES AND THE COURTS

The staffs of federal and state civil rights agencies and the courts are not well qualified to assess and decide the relative competencies and promise of individual teacher-scholars for a particular tenure position at a university. They lack the long years of academic experience and the professional knowledge in the academic subfields. Therefore, alleged cases of discrimination in promotion or appointment to a tenure position are difficult for them to handle with assurance. They can, presumably, make some judgment regarding the adequacy of the recruitment, of the information available, and of the procedures followed.

For the staffs of government agencies and the courts to review

[5] Increased to 1,500 by April 1974.

[6] A tenure position at a major university usually means a professor's salary and benefits for 30 to 35 years, which is roughly the yearly income from (say) $600,000 of capital funds.

in open hearings the validity of appointment, promotion, and salary decisions made under the procedures explained in Chapter 2 raises other serious issues. Under assurance of strictly confidential use in order to encourage candor, assessments by distinguished teacher-scholars are obtained comparing the complainant's qualifications for a position or promotion to tenure with other faculty at that university and elsewhere. To reveal such confidential assessments as comparative evidence in open hearings or in court would not only discourage frank assessments in the future but also would involve invasion of the privacy of persons not directly party to the case and could seriously injure their professional reputations.

In addition, the tenured members of a department, members of ad hoc or standing faculty committees, and academic administrators could be required to testify as to their group discussions and decisions concerning the faculty member and to testify in detail about the weaknesses and strengths of various candidates and about past mistakes made in promotion to tenure. Such a requirement would discourage candid judgments in the future because of possible exposure in hearings and thus would reduce the effectiveness of evaluative procedures. It would also tend to discourage use of the principle of salary increases according to merit and would encourage automatic and uniform increases or increases according to length of service in the rank or some other formula applied without direct relationship to performance. Small differences in salary increase might seem too difficult to explain with several persons participating in the decision.

For these reasons, reliance on statistics to determine the existence or nonexistence of discrimination in faculty employment could be quite incorrect and actually misleading. Unverifiable claims that particular statements were made in conversation between the complainant and, say, the departmental chairman can make a case seem to rest heavily on one person's word against another's. Therefore, there is a need to reduce to writing messages to individual faculty about the quality of their work and for department chairmen and deans to maintain written summaries of meetings where statements and evaluations of a faculty member's performance and prospects are made.

Adversary proceedings between a faculty member and a university—which are really directed mainly at those faculty who participated in the evaluations and decisions alleged to be discriminatory—that take place in open hearings held by a government agency or in court can cause lasting rifts and bitterness in a department, especially where faculty enjoy academic freedom and tenure and the department is largely self-governing.

The faculty of major universities are but a very small fraction of the total employment covered either by Revised Order No. 4[7] or by the Civil Rights Act of 1964 as amended. The danger to the universities is that federal and state rules, agency decisions, and federal and state court decisions will be based on the industrial model of employment and management and will fail to make proper allowance for university faculty systems of shared government, academic freedom plus academic tenure, and compensation and advancement according to evaluations of a candidate's performance and potential as a faculty member and contributor to progress in that field or subfield, made by mature teacher-scholars.

With the quality of a department and the university so importantly involved in making tenure appointments, government-agency and court decisions based on the industry model could have profound implications for the faculties of major universities.

EXPOSURE TO CHARGES

Experience clearly demonstrates that a university invites charges of discrimination whenever it deviates in a faculty appointment or promotion from the principle of selecting the candidate properly judged to be the best qualified to fulfill the requirements of the position. The same is true for the determination of individual salaries. Selection and reward according to individual performance and future promise based on past performance are basic for achieving equal employment opportunity, for providing proper incentives for accomplishment, and for maintaining the integrity of the institution.

Presumably the federal and state agencies and courts, in judging the validity of individual complaints of discrimination, should use that same standard. Both prejudice against, and preference for, persons on the basis of color, race, sex, or other nonperformance attributes are destructive of equal employment opportunity.

A university by its very nature may be especially vulnerable to a

[7] Under the Executive orders, every enterprise with over 50 employees that has a federal contract or subcontracts totaling $50,000 must have a written affirmative action program for each of its establishments; every institution or organization holding a federal contract or subcontract of $10,000 or more must agree not to discriminate against any employee or applicant for employment with respect to race, color, religion, sex, or national origin.

charge of discrimination both for and against faculty on such grounds as race, religion, sex, or national origin. Faculty are encouraged, by academic freedom and tenure and by academic training, to be independent thinkers and to explore various ideas and systems of thought. The classroom is a place for examining differing and conflicting views. It is not that faculty are especially bias-prone but only that they do and should express themselves freely in seminars, classes, and department or committee meetings.

The tenured members of a department usually play a key role in the selection and advancement of department faculty. Therefore, what one or more of them may say or write in letters, articles, private conversation, or the classroom may possibly be allowed as evidence of bias in an open hearing held by an agency or in a court. It is possible, therefore, that the adjudication of an individual complaint could raise a serious question concerning academic freedom and tenure as well as confidentiality of solicited letters of evaluation. In addition, apparently there is no time limit on the filing of discrimination charges or the distance back in time that statements and events can be used in such proceedings as evidence of personal bias on grounds of race, sex, religion, and national origin.

CONSEQUENCES OF GOVERNMENT PROSECUTION AND ADJUDICATION

It will be useful to explain in summary fashion the various short-run and long-term disadvantages to the parties that resort to government agency or court procedures for settlement may involve.

1 Once a complaint is filed with a federal or state agency or a court and a formal statement setting forth the alleged discrimination is presented to the institution, forces are set in motion on both sides aimed at preparing the strongest possible position. Both sides are likely to put their case in the hands of a lawyer, who will view the matter in the light of past court decisions, effective evidence, and legal tactics. Stress is put on arguing and winning the case.

2 With the complaint filed and lawyers working on the preparation and presentation of their case, things begin to happen to faculty relations in the department and the university. Faculty and administrators are cautioned on what they can and should say, because the complaint normally would be against a recommendation or decision by the tenured members of the department concerning the complainant's appointment, reappointment, promotion, or salary and

also presumably against action taken by any faculty or faculty-administration committee that reviews and acts on department recommendations. Tensions rise and sides are taken by faculty, administrators, and students, with publicity about the case appearing in the student paper and other media. (Some 400 female employees at the University of Pennsylvania are said to contribute to the legal expenses of women filing a sex discrimination case against the institution.)

3 The processing of a case by a civil rights agency or a court usually takes considerable time because of a backlog of cases. Often the preparation and presentation of the case are fairly expensive in terms of effort, money, and psychological wear and tear on the parties. Open hearings held by an agency or by a court tend to create tension and bitterness within the complainant's department and the university, as the tenured members of the department and members of the review committee testify and are cross-examined concerning the basis for their decisions with respect to the complainant's appointment and pay. Comparisons are likely to be drawn in terms of strengths, weaknesses, and rate of progress of faculty in the same or a higher rank in the department and in similar departments such as foreign languages and literatures. Use in public hearings of information and evaluations of other faculty for comparison with the complainant's qualities as a teacher, scholar, and colleague, and skill in administering programs is likely to be embarrassing to both the complainant and faculty used for such comparative purposes. If outside letters of evaluation have been obtained under promise of confidentiality, any requirement to reveal their contents in such hearings not only could be embarrassing but also could result in inability of the institution henceforth to obtain such valuable candid assessments.

4 A decision by a government agency or a court could be unsatisfactory to both parties. That is not too unlikely because agency staffs and judges cannot be expected to be highly knowledgeable concerning faculty practices and problems and are likely in decisions to follow precedents in cases decided according to the industry model rather than the academic-faculty model of operation. A decision may build in bitterness and conflict that will seriously hamper the effectiveness of the department and its members long into the future. Certain kinds of decisions could almost assure continued discord and subsequent filing of new charges of discrimination.

Because of the likelihood of such difficulties and disadvantages to the parties in cases processed through the agencies and the courts, it would be desirable if the parties had an option to use, if both wished to do so, a method of dispute settlement that might be more satisfactory, especially for faculty cases.

OUTSIDE MEDIATION-ARBITRATION

In view of the possible unsatisfactory consequences of processing faculty complaints of discrimination through government agencies and the courts, an optional alternative procedure is proposed for voluntary use where it is appropriate. Compared with agency-court processing of discrimination complaints, the optional procedure would, for many cases: (1) be quicker and less costly, (2) use persons who understand how universities do and should operate for factual investigation, mediation, and settlement decisions, (3) provide better assessment of the validity and value of comparative data and statements, without the necessity of faculty colleagues having to present, in open meeting, detailed assessments of the strengths and weaknesses of the complainant compared with others in the department and elsewhere, in terms of teaching, research, and general usefulness and value to the university, (4) be more likely to result in a mutually acceptable settlement through mediation (conciliation) than would be the case if handled by a government civil rights agency, and (5) where an outside decision is necessary, result in one that is more likely to be mutually face-saving and satisfactory to both parties over the long run.[8]

The essence of the proposal is to provide to the parties a choice of submitting a claim of discrimination in faculty employment that cannot be settled by means of internal procedures, to outside investigation, mediation, and, if necessary, arbitration. The mediator-arbitrators would be selected by the parties from a panel composed

[8] In deciding on a remedy in the case of university faculty, account usually would need to be taken of the existence of specialization by subfield, the fact that only one expert may be needed in many subfields, and the practice of professors having continuing tenure. Such factors may sharply restrict transfer to another position and create the possibility of repeated appeals to the court over an extended period of time, whereas in industry there would generally be much more flexibility of adjustment to a court order to rehire or promote an employee.

of faculty members at a number of institutions, most of whom would have had experience as labor arbitrators. The component parts of the proposal can be explained as follows:

1 Arrangements would be made for a public-service agency, with interest in the mediation and arbitration of disputes, to administer such a program. One suggested agency is the National Center for Dispute Settlement, a division of the American Arbitration Association. Established in mid-1968, with headquarters in Washington and local operations in eight cities across the country, it has been engaged in developing ways of providing third-party neutral assistance for resolving community, consumer, public-employment, and similar types of conflict through the services of experienced mediators and arbitrators.

2 The program could begin to operate either with a national panel of 100 to 200 faculty mediator-arbitrators and with selected universities and colleges around the country participating, or on a regional unit basis, with regional panels of faculty mediator-arbitrators and with participation by selected universities and colleges in the regional area. Examples of such regional areas are the following: the area within 100 miles of Boston, the New York–Philadelphia regional area, the area within 150 or 200 miles of Chicago, the area between Washington, D.C., and Durham–Chapel Hill in North Carolina, and the area between San Francisco and Los Angeles in California.

3 Persons named to a national or regional panel would be tenured faculty with sufficient independence, academic reputation, and (in most cases) arbitration experience, so that their investigation and mediation efforts and their arbitration decisions would be well respected. Because there is an insufficient number of experienced female and minority-group faculty members for such a program, it would be necessary to provide for the development of a more adequate supply. To some extent, that could be accomplished by having some of them gain experience by participating with others on individual cases.

4 At least in the early experimental stages, the cost of financing mediation-arbitration in each case (arbitrator's fees, travel, overhead) would be met by payment of at least half the cost by the institution. The remainder hopefully would be covered, at least

for an experimental period, by foundation support and possibly other sources. The complainant charging sex or race discrimination in employment could not be expected to pay part of such costs because he or she can have the case prosecuted free of charge by federal and state agencies. It might prove desirable to have some means of making sure that complaints submitted to the procedure actually should have that treatment, particularly if the costless aspect encouraged many requests for use of the method where that seemed unnecessary.

5 Outside mediator-arbitrators should have the right to examine all pertinent material, including confidential letters of evaluation, to interview all persons involved in the matter or useful for comparative purposes, and to obtain confidential assessments of their own. Private hearings would be usually held, with stress placed on getting all the facts in a calm, objective manner, without any publicity. Lawyers would not be necessary in many cases. In such ways, hostility and bitterness could be minimized.

6 After obtaining and assessing all the facts, the mediator-arbitrator(s) could talk tentatively with both parties separately about the directions that their thinking was taking and what those directions might imply with respect to a decision. Under such circumstances, a mediated settlement might be more possible than if a federal or state agency (the prosecutor) were to try to mediate the dispute.

7 A decision by the mediator-arbitrator(s) would be considered conclusive, unless the parties stipulated otherwise or court action modified or nullified the decision. In some cases, a university may be reluctant to allow outside arbitrators to grant continuous tenure as part of a binding arbitration decision. However, a complainant may insist, as a condition of entering the procedure, that the mediator-arbitrator(s) have the same power to levy remedies as a federal or state agency and the courts. Such conditions can be spelled out in the stipulation to arbitrate.

8 The procedures and decisions of mediator-arbitrator(s) can be more flexible and better adapted to the circumstances of the case and the academic department involved than would be the situation under agency and court action. Therefore, in many cases it is likely that a decision by faculty arbitrators would be more constructive over the long run than decisions handed down, after public adversary proceedings, by government agencies and the courts. An agency or court decision would be more likely to be based on precedents developed in previous cases on the basis of industrial employment conditions.[9]

9 Either party would be free to agree to enter or decline to enter this sort of ad hoc arrangement for outside faculty mediation-arbitration, and each would be free to choose (say) one mediator-arbitrator from the panel, with a third panel member chosen by those two, by lot, or by some other means. In any decision, the mediator-arbitrators chosen would be constrained by the terms of stipulation to arbitrate drawn up and agreed to by the parties.

With a few exceptions, the proposal has met with a favorable response from university faculty, administrators, and representatives of women and minority groups. Its advantages in reducing the delay, bitterness, and costliness of alternative methods and the advantages of private handling of such cases by knowledgeable faculty from outside are well understood by persons who have had experience with a case carried through an agency procedure and the courts.

Discussion of the proposal with a variety of persons, including arbitrators and law professors, has indicated a number of possible problems that might develop. It would, therefore, seem best to start on a relatively small scale in selected areas in an experimental manner.

Some possible problems can be briefly indicated. One is that such an arrangement might encourage an unnecessarily large volume of complaints to be handled by that means. If experience so indicated, there might be a need, say, to develop some sort of advisory service by sympathetic faculty to help screen out complaints that need not or should not be submitted to the outside mediation-arbitration process.

Another problem could be the development of a sufficient number of tenured female and minority-group faculty as mediator-arbitrators. Some universities (for example, Cornell, UCLA, Berkeley) have programs for training arbitrators. However, in most cases,

[9] The significance of the application of the industrial model of employment to faculty may be indicated by the following provision in Revised Order No. 4, par. 60-2.24 (f)(s): "Neither minority nor female employees should be required to possess higher qualifications than those of the lowest qualified incumbent." It is rather surprising to find that provision cited with approval for application to university faculty in an article that also states that the regulations regarding promotion in Revised Order No. 4 "strengthen merit standards." See Weitzman (1973, pp. 472, 484).

working with faculty experienced in mediation-arbitration should provide the principal component of training for faculty who initially may lack such experience. The panel from which a mediator-arbitrator or, say, three mediator-arbitrators are selected should be large enough to provide adequate choice and to keep the demand for any one person's service under the plan within reasonable bounds.

A third problem is illustrated by the U.S. Supreme Court's decision in *Alexander v. Gardner-Denver Co.* (decided February 19, 1974).[10] The decision in that case held that an employee's submission of his claim to final arbitration under a nondiscrimination clause of a collective-bargaining agreement does not foreclose his statutory right to a trial *de novo* under Title VII of the Civil Rights Act of 1964. In considering an employee's claim in a court action, "the federal court may admit the arbitral decision as evidence and accord it such weight as may be appropriate under the facts and circumstances of each case."

The Supreme Court points out that "presumably an employee may waive his" right of court action under Title VII as part of a voluntary settlement and that arbitration "may satisfy an employee's perceived need to resort to the judicial forum, thus saving" both parties the costs and aggravations associated with a lawsuit.

The mediation-arbitration proposal presented here differs in a number of respects from arbitration of a grievance under a collective-bargaining agreement. Under such an agreement, the grievance procedure and the arbitrator are predetermined by the management and the union; the union may not have a significant interest in representing the rights of the grievant under antidiscrimination legislation; and the arbitrator is supposed to interpret and apply the collective-bargaining agreement in ruling on the complaint.

The mediation-arbitration proposal for faculty is not subject to those constraints. The parties are free to use or not to use this means for resolving the complaint. They participate in the selection of the mediator-arbitrator(s) on an ad hoc basis for this particular case. The mediator-arbitrator(s) are subject to the stipulation to arbitrate, which the parties agreed upon to govern the arbitration process and to be the basis for an award. The case is directly concerned with an issue of discrimination in employment alleged to be

[10] For the full text of the decision, see *Daily Labor Report* (1974).

on grounds of race, sex, religion, or national origin as specified in the federal and state legislation. Thus the rights of the complainant under Title VII of the Civil Rights Act and under state fair employment practices laws would be taken into account in a mediated settlement or an arbitration award.[11]

Presumably such factors would be taken into account by the federal courts, should individuals bring a Title VII suit following a decision under the program of outside mediation-arbitration for faculty. Also, that program should considerably reduce resort to court action. Nevertheless the decision in *Alexander v. Gardner-Denver Co.* (1974) clearly indicates that the federal courts have the ultimate powers to enforce Title VII. That fact would need to be taken into account in designing and operating the mediation-arbitration program.

The financing of the program beyond the first year or two could present a problem. It has been suggested that universities and colleges might be willing to pay most or all of the cost of operation. Full payment by the institution, however, could raise an objection that such financing might possibly affect the outcome of the process. Perhaps it would be desirable to experiment in one area to see whether that sort of objection has any validity. Undoubtedly, partial support could be developed from outside sources if the total was not a large sum.

In the operation of a new program, of course, unanticipated problems are bound to arise. Many would be administrative in character.

The benefits of such a program have, for the most part, been already explained. They are the effective operation of the faculty systems of self-government and reward according to merit as determined by professional evaluation, relatively prompt enforcement of justice and rectification of injustice in faculty affairs, and effective operation of academic departments. The development and operation of such a program would present university faculty and administrators with the opportunity and challenge to work out the necessary adaptations of their systems of government and justice for faculty to meet changing conditions and developments in public policy.

[11] One might also observe again that a large part of the total university faculty in the country, both male and female, are, according to surveys, very sympathetic to fair, and even preferential, treatment of minority persons and women in faculty employment.

7. Administration of Regulations and Laws

Federal and state agencies have had difficulties in trying to administer their enforcement programs as applied to university faculty. Several factors help to explain their difficulties.

Generally, the enforcement programs are not altogether clear concerning their short-run and long-run objectives. As previously explained, the HEW program of contract compliance tries to pursue two objectives that are not fully consistent: nondiscrimination and pressures to favor racial minority groups and women, on grounds that persons belonging to those categories have in the past suffered from discrimination in many kinds of employment. In addition to such inconsistency, the HEW Guidelines (based on Revised Order No. 4) are, as has been pointed out, ill-suited for much faculty employment. Consequently, as is explained more fully below, HEW's 10 civil rights regional offices are uneven in their interpretations and in their demands with respect to items to be included in affirmative action plans and the depth of intrusion into a university's internal operations. Also, university faculty are so unusual in their methods of operation that the staffs of federal and state compliance agencies encounter difficulties when they try to apply uniformly to universities the program rules and assumptions that grow out of conditions in industry and construction or even public grade and high schools or hospitals. Most members of the staffs of compliance agencies have had little experience as regular faculty members or academic administrators in a university. Without such experience they may not be well qualified for the task of developing appropriate applications of complicated rules and statistical calculations to the special circumstances of faculty operations.

For an institution to be in compliance, its affirmative action plan must be acceptable to the HEW Office for Civil Rights. Under delegation from the Director of the Office of Federal Contract Compliance in the Department of Labor, the Office for Civil Rights in HEW has the power to issue special rules and regulations to apply to universities and colleges, to conduct compliance reviews, and to approve or disapprove written affirmative action plans of colleges and universities. Such HEW approval, or HEW disapproval that leads to withdrawal of federal contract eligibility, is subject to review and confirmation by the Department of Labor. Thus, the HEW Office for Civil Rights has responsibility for determining in the first instance whether a contractor is in compliance or is able to comply as the result of the submission of an acceptable affirmative action plan. The extent to which one of HEW's regional offices has the authority to approve or disapprove of a proposed affirmative action plan seems to have varied from time to time. In 1973 regional offices apparently had the power to disapprove a plan but could only recommend approval to the Washington headquarters. If a proposal raises an issue or issues that have not been decided in rulings already made, the matter is submitted to HEW headquarters in Washington and, if necessary, to the Department of Labor, for ultimate determination.

In case a university or college is found to be in noncompliance, HEW's Office for Civil Rights recommends to the Department of Labor possible enforcement action, which would normally take the form of placing the institution on complete or partial ineligibility for new contracts or renewal of existing contracts. Authority for such action rests in the Department of Labor. As indicated in Chapter 1, by the end of 1973 some 20 universities had been subjected to a temporary block of new contracts or renewals, on grounds of noncompliance. In the case of universities and colleges, the federal government has not proceeded to the stage of formal termination of a contract or formal ineligibility proceedings.[1]

Largely because compliance reviews, approval and disapproval of university affirmative action plans, and prosecution of individual complaints by EEOC and state agencies each come up one university at a time, the administration of government enforcement agencies and programs has not had an objective, critical review by scholars. No such careful review and analysis are attempted here.

[1] Disapprovals of proposed affirmative action plans generally mean further negotiation of a plan that is acceptable. Depending on the circumstances, an institution could be declared ineligible for contract renewal or new contracts while negotiations about revisions of its proposed affirmative action program are proceeding.

It is necessary, however, to pay some attention to administrative problems, because the difficulties they raise are important for understanding the need for serious reworking of the HEW Guidelines.

THE STAFFS OF ENFORCEMENT AGENCIES

The staff of HEW engaged in compliance enforcement for institutions of higher education is quite small when one considers the tasks that enforcement of the HEW Guidelines presumably involve. As of June 30, 1973, a total of 74 persons were engaged in compliance reviews, in criticism and decisions with respect to affirmative action plans presented by colleges and universities, and in other aspects of enforcement. Of the 74 total, 16 were in the Washington headquarters and 58 in the 10 regional offices, ranging from 10 in the New York and Atlanta offices to 3 in the Philadelphia and the Seattle offices. No one was reported as officially assigned to the Higher Education Division in the Kansas City office. In regional offices there may be some temporary shifting of personnel between divisions (for example, from elementary and secondary education and vice versa) as the need requires.[2]

The size of the staff has remained fairly constant since the Higher Education Division was established in April 1972. However, significant changes in personnel have occurred in several of the regional offices in the past three years. In fact, the turnover in some regional offices has been extremely high, with staff members leaving for higher pay in industry. For example, of the staff of seven in the Chicago office in November 1973, only one had been there in 1970.

Women and especially blacks are overrepresented among the 74 staff members in the Higher Education Division. On June 30, 1973, about one-half (35) were women, almost three-fifths (43) were members of minorities, and approximately one-half (35) were blacks. The 58 regional compliance officers were distributed as follows: 25 women (13 blacks, 10 whites, and 2 members of other minorities) and 33 males (13 blacks, 14 whites, and 6 members of other minorities).

The level of staff appointments for the 58 in the field is not, for the group as a whole, very high. At the end of June 1973, some two-thirds (40) were in grades G.S. 11 to 14 (minimum basic

[2] Data on the Higher Education Division staff are provided in a letter (with 12 pages of tables) from Gweldolyn H. Gregory, Director of Office of Policy Communication, Office for Civil Rights, HEW, to Sheldon E. Steinbach, American Council on Education, dated Sept. 17, 1973.

salaries for the first year from around $14,000 to $23,000);[3] the other third (18) were in grades G.S. 6 to 9 (minimum basic salaries for the first year from around $8,500 to $11,600).

On June 30, 1973, blacks occupied the top positions in the Higher Education Division in the following major regional offices: Boston, New York, Philadelphia, Atlanta, Chicago, and San Francisco. Blacks were in grade 14 in four of those offices; a black and a white shared the highest grade of 13 in the Chicago office; and a black was acting head as a grade 12 in the Philadelphia office. In addition, blacks were in the grade just below the top grade as follows: 1 out of 2 in Boston, 1 out of 2 in New York, 3 out of 7 in Atlanta, 2 out of 2 in Chicago, and 1 out of 4 in San Francisco. The blacks holding the high-level positions in the regional offices have come heavily from the civil rights movement.

Women held high positions in the Higher Education Division in regional offices as follows: 1 out of 2 in the highest grade in Chicago and second highest in grade level among the Higher Education Division staff in 1 out of 2 persons in Boston and in New York, 1 out of 1 in Philadelphia, and 2 out of 7 in Atlanta.

Just how much blacks and women are overrepresented on the higher education staff in the regional offices (and white males are underrepresented) may be difficult to determine. Here also there is a problem of how to define and measure the pool of available and qualified persons for the field staff of the Higher Education Division of HEW's Office for Civil Rights. However, it would be difficult by any definition to conclude that the staff of mid-1973 was proportional by race or sex to the pool of qualified persons.

There would seem to have been a conscious attempt to achieve overrepresentation of blacks and women, and to do so even though the resulting staff was generally deficient in background experience and detailed knowledge about the systems of faculty self-determination and governance in American universities. Lack of full understanding of the peculiarities of university operations apparently helps to explain why some of the demands of regional offices have been inappropriate and why university officials have experienced some difficulties in communicating with HEW regional personnel.

Only 14 of the 74 staff at headquarters or in the field are reported to have had some experience in the faculty or in the administrative or consultative positions in a college or university. Few have had

[3] Seven were in grade 14, 10 in grade 13, 14 in grade 12, and 9 in grade 11. The salary schedule for federal employees was raised effective October 1, 1973.

extensive experience in a university as a member of a faculty or the academic administration. In an effort to help remedy such deficiencies in the staff, various three-day seminars or training programs have been held, and new employees in regional offices are considered for the first three months to be in an orientation-training program under the auspices of the regional branch chief.

It would be desirable for the staff to have more understanding and appreciation of (1) the importance of independence and diversity for university educational programs, (2) the need for considerable involvement of faculty in university governance and managerial responsibilities and what that implies for compliance enforcement, (3) the vital significance of maintaining merit as the main basis for faculty selection and individual salaries, (4) the characteristics of faculty labor supply by discipline and subfield and by type of institution, and (5) the differences between tenure and nontenure positions in terms of supply, demand, and responsibilities in different departments and universities. Also, some training in statistical analysis and labor market analysis would be helpful. Lack of such background and understanding is evident in the demands and comments that the compliance staff make and the rather rigid manner in which, in some cases in particular regions, the inappropriate language and concepts of Revised Order No. 4 are rigidly applied to university faculties.

The staffs of EEOC and the state civil rights agencies are likely to be even less conscious of the implications for compliance enforcement of the professional practices and the collegial methods of decision making in universities. Also, the compliance thinking in those agencies is more likely to be influenced by legal concerns and decisions in previous court cases arising in manufacturing and other lines of business. The field staff of the Department of Labor's Wage-Hour Division, which investigates for violations of the Equal Pay Act, likewise tends to think in terms of conditions and practices that have prevailed in industry over a long period of time.

DECISIONS ON AFFIRMATIVE ACTION PLANS

The Higher Education Division of HEW's Office for Civil Rights has been slow in approving or disapproving affirmative action plans. Some universities have waited a year or more after submitting a plan without learning whether it is considered approvable or not. Also some regional offices have rejected a surprisingly high proportion of the affirmative action plans submitted to them.

Table 8 contains interesting information with respect to the

TABLE 8
HEW action on affirmative action plans of colleges and universities, by regions,* November 16, 1971 through December 31, 1972

Regional office	*Plans submitted*	*Plans given interim or final approval*	*Plans rejected*	*Plans pending*
Boston	16	1	0	15
New York	31	1	13	17
Philadelphia	4	1	0	3
Atlanta	12	0	6	6
Chicago	24	0	0	24
Dallas	25	11	5	9
Kansas City	11	0	11	0
Denver	34	8	5	21
San Francisco	32	7	8	17
Seattle	8	1	3	4
TOTAL	197	30	51	116

* Coverage of regional offices: (I) Boston—Massachusetts, Connecticut, Maine, New Hampshire, Rhode Island, Vermont; (II) New York City—New York, New Jersey, Puerto Rico, Virgin Islands; (III) Philadelphia—Pennsylvania, Maryland, West Virginia, Virginia; (IV) Atlanta—Georgia, Alabama, Florida, Kentucky, Mississippi, North Carolina, South Carolina, Tennessee; (V) Chicago—Illinois, Ohio, Indiana, Michigan, Wisconsin; (VI) Dallas—Arkansas, Louisiana, Oklahoma, Texas, New Mexico; (VII) Kansas City—Missouri, Iowa, Kansas, Nebraska; (VIII) Denver—Colorado, Utah, Wyoming, North and South Dakota, Montana; (IX) San Francisco—California, Nevada, Arizona; (X) Seattle—Washington, Oregon, Idaho.

SOURCE: Letter to Sheldon Steinbach of the American Council on Education from Gwendolyn H. Gregory, Director of Office of Policy Communication, Office for Civil Rights, HEW, dated Sept. 17, 1973.

concentrated character of the HEW enforcement program among the nation's 916 institutions of higher education that are said to be subject to federal contract compliance. Up to the end of 1972, only 30 plans had been approved and 26 of them were in three regions: Dallas, Denver, and San Francisco. The Chicago regional office had not formally approved or disapproved any plans, although some had been reviewed and 24 were pending. The Kansas City office had rejected 11 plans and approved none, and had none pending (presumably under review); New York had accepted one and rejected 13.[4] The rejection rate is surprisingly high—51 out of 81 plans. Such unevenness in the record can be explained in part by the circumstances in the HEW regional offices, such as

[4] The author was unable to obtain full confirmation of these figures at the New York regional office, and at least two universities claim to have had affirmative action plans accepted by the New York regional office during that period. The San Francisco office claims that no plans have been approved since December 1971 so that the figure in Table 8 is questionable.

turnover of personnel and different conceptions of the requirements for an approvable plan.

Furthermore, during the seven months from January 1, 1973, to July 23, 1973, only three additional affirmative action plans were given approval by the 10 regional offices. The other 115 that were pending at the end of 1972 were either rejected or were still pending. That is remarkably slow action. It might seem to indicate that the affirmative action plans submitted by colleges and universities are being generally subjected to fairly exacting requirements, but partly it is due to lack of expertise sufficient to judge the validity of goals and other technical aspects of the plans submitted.

The distribution of the power of approval and disapproval of affirmative action plans between the regional offices and the Washington headquarters remains unclear. The impression has been given that considerable decentralization of authority has occurred, yet letters to university presidents are said to have been held for as long as three months in Washington for official clearance. Certainly there is significant variation in enforcement demands and in decisions on affirmative action plans among the regions, apparently due in part to the personal characteristics of the leadership in the regional offices.

The instructions that regional enforcement officials give universities and colleges in connection with the findings of a compliance review, the development of an affirmative action plan, and the rejection of affirmative action plans are based on the HEW Guidelines and Revised Order No. 4. On the basis of the experience of many universities, a letter from the regional director of the Office for Civil Rights of HEW to the president of a university rejecting its affirmative action plan as submitted might include such statements (in part, "demands")[5] as the following:

1. The main reason for rejection of the ____________ University's affirmative action plan is lack of the required utilization analysis for female and minority-group personnel necessary to determine deficiencies and to establish goals and timetables by department or organizational unit for the elimination of all deficiencies. Your affirmative action plan must address itself to each item in Revised Order No. 4. Each department chairman

[5] The word "demands" is used here in a labor relations sense, because there may be some leeway or margin for "negotiations" if the university can give good reasons for its position or can explain why the requests of the regional director are not reasonable or are inappropriate.

and other officer with hiring authority is required to determine availability data for women and minorities in each discipline.

2. The required utilization analysis is necessary to determine whether goals and timetables have been accurately drawn. The Higher Education Guidelines provide that goals should be set in order to overcome identified deficiencies "within a reasonable time." In Appendix J the guidelines state: "In many cases this can be accomplished within 5 years; in others more time or less time will be required." The goals and timetables to overcome underutilization in a particular organization unit must reflect not only the number of new hires but also the projected overall composition of the faculty in that unit.

3. Provide an organizational chart covering all operations of the university. Detail all lines of authority and link the various levels of supervisory authority as they relate to employment.

4. Clearly set forth the roles, relationships, and authority of the university's affirmative action officer. Section 41CFR60-2.22 of Revised Order No. 4 delineates the duties with which the affirmative action officer should be charged. The affirmative action plan should set forth the responsibility of the affirmative action officer for monitoring such aspects of the affirmative action plan as new hires and promotion and tenure decisions.

5. Give the function, authority, and composition by race and sex of all university committees and the provision for equitable representation of the protected class members on such committees. The equal employment opportunity (EEO) committee should have the same type of authority in administering the affirmative action plan as other committees have in administering their respective programs.

6. It is necessary to develop and validate a full job description for each category of employee including faculty.

7. Give a detailed explanation of the criteria used and their relative weighting for appointment and promotion of each category of employee including faculty.

8. All selection criteria and techniques for assessing qualifications must be validated to prove that they clearly relate to job performance and do not have an adverse impact on women or minorities. Such validation is required by Revised Order No. 4.[6]

9. Analyze the composition of applicant flow by minority-group status and sex.

[6] Revised Order No. 4 (Title 41, Code of Federal Regulations, Part 60-3, Oct. 2, 1971, in the *Federal Register*) sets forth a definition of selection "tests" that includes various selection techniques, including "casual interviews" and "unscored personal history and background requirements," for which validation

10. Analyze the number of women and minorities considered for and granted tenure compared with nonminority faculty in the same classifications in order to make certain that women and minorities have equal opportunity for tenure.

11. Provide that the work performance of all supervisory personnel should be evaluated on the basis of their EEO efforts and results, with sanctions for failure to adhere to equal employment principles.

12. Before a contractor can be found in compliance with the executive order, it must make a specific commitment, in writing, indicating the specific steps it will take to correct any and all deficiencies. The affirmative action plan of ____________ University must fulfill that requirement in order to be approved.

Certain conclusions can be drawn from such statements. One, HEW enforcement officers generally think and act within the framework of the concepts and requirements of Revised Order No. 4, on which the HEW Guidelines are based. Their efforts are to a considerable extent directed at inducing universities and colleges to have their operations, including faculty, conform to the industry pattern of authority, employment practices, and personnel management.

Two, HEW enforcement officers in some regions seek to make numerical goals and timetables by department or "hiring unit" a key element in affirmative action programs, including for faculty, regardless of the size or appropriateness of the department. The authority structure they tend to favor conflicts with the collegial or faculty system of shared responsibility in decision making by mature teacher-scholars. The HEW enforcement officers, interested in certain results more than in procedures to assure the best professional judgments, seem desirous of enhancing the authority of a university's newly appointed equal employment opportunity officers and coordinators, who, for the most part, have not been drawn from the faculty and are not responsible to the faculty.

Three, the HEW enforcement officers seek to induce greater use of women and members of minorities on committees, in administrative activities, and in other internal governmental functions.

---

may be necessary. Where there are "data suggesting the possibility of discrimination, such as higher rates of rejection of minority candidates than of nonminority candidates for the same job" or where there is "underutilization" of minority-group personnel in certain types of jobs, validation studies must be made or the conditions suggestive of employment discrimination must be eliminated.

They apparently do not appreciate that heavy involvement in such activities can significantly reduce the time and effort that a faculty member is able to devote to teaching and scholarship and, thus, can have adverse effects on their qualifications for advancement as teacher-scholars.

Four, the HEW enforcement officials apparently do not appreciate that some of the instructions they give universities (based on the industrial model of Revised Order No. 4) are not appropriate for a system of faculty self-government. Partly for that reason, the data are costly to develop.

Five, through their power to approve or disapprove affirmative action plans, HEW enforcement officials are, either consciously or unconsciously, attempting to alter the structure of authority and governance in universities in line with the industrial model embodied in Revised Order No. 4. In doing so, they are tending to undermine faculty self-government, to create conflicts of group interest within universities and, as was explained in the preceding chapter, to expose universities to new liabilities under the federal and state antidiscrimination laws.

Six, too often the resulting provisions in an institutions's affirmative action plan are the result of negotiations by persons with different conceptions and objectives. The resulting document is, therefore, likely to be a compromise between university principles and government guidelines.

It is said that HEW enforcement activities have led to improvements in the industrial relations programs of universities, especially for nonacademic personnel, for whom universities have had to modernize their programs of personnel management. That is true in many cases, and undoubtedly represents some benefit or improvement in certain institutions. However, one should not overlook the costs involved in preparing and negotiating approvable affirmative action plans and the effects that government regulation seems likely to have on the effective operation of universities in the long run if present policies continue.

The kinds of programs for governance and for staffing decisions that universities should have in academic and in nonacademic operations is a question that neither the universities nor the government have fully analyzed and answered. It is becoming more and more difficult to maintain a significant difference between the academic system and the system of hierarchical authority in nonacademic employment. This subject is considered in some detail in the next chapter.

THE INCREASING INTRICACY OF REGULATION

For individual universities, each successive affirmative action plan is much longer, more detailed, and more interventionist than the previous one. Disapproval of a plan inevitably means that the university is instructed to provide a still more elaborate plan, and approvals are often accompanied by instructions to supply even more details and additional provisions of substance.

Expansion of government regulation is almost an inevitable development. Growth in regulatory activity is especially likely to occur with respect to faculty employment in major universities because the HEW civil rights officials are trying (1) to apply the industrial model to university faculty where it does not fit, (2) to determine "deficiencies in the hiring and promotion of minorities and women" by a technique that in practice has serious deficiencies for that purpose, (3) to use a concession negotiated at one university as a pattern to spread to others, and (4) to alter the distribution of influence and authority for faculty hiring and promotion in line with the concepts and assumptions of Revised Order No. 4.

The way that regulation tends to expand can be illustrated by an example. On May 1, 1973, Harvard submitted to the HEW regional office its third affirmative action plan. The previous two had been submitted in February 1970 and November 1971. In mid-June, Harvard received word that this plan was rejected as "inadequate and unresponsive to the Executive order," because it did not include a "utilization analysis" and a numerical goal for each of 30-odd departments in the arts and sciences. Harvard then submitted at the end of July a five-volume plan in line with the HEW instructions.

In mid-November, the HEW regional office notified Harvard that its plan was "an acceptable standard upon which the University can build and implement an effective affirmative action program" (*Harvard University Gazette,* 1973). However, HEW asked Harvard to develop and submit material on 10 items "for future inclusion" in its plan with a view to "building a truly comprehensive program." Among the 10 items (all said to be "required by Revised Order No. 4") were the following five:

1. Develop a Salary Equity Analysis as per Attachment [see Exhibit 1] for Minorities and Women.

2. Develop and submit job descriptions for every category of employment, especially for Exempt Employees and for Faculty by Department where these have not been previously submitted.

3. Develop and submit detailed criteria for selection and promotion for

each job category and for faculty by rank by department where these have not been previously submitted.

4. Validate all tests presently used in selection, upgrading, or promotion.

5. Develop a comprehensive program to increase the number of minority and female contractors and vendors.

By requiring the first four items, HEW is insisting that the techniques of job analysis and evaluation used in industry be applied to the hiring, promotion, and pay for Harvard faculty in the arts and sciences where they are not likely to be appropriate. As explained in Chapters 2 and 3, the tenured faculty of a leading university like Harvard are usually hired and paid on the basis of their personal distinction as teacher-scholars in their fields and not according to the contents of their "job." Their job content could be essentially the same as that of a number of assistant professors in the same department or the university. If detailed job descriptions are requested, they might be different for each faculty member and change as his or her teaching and research changed. Such detailed descriptions would indicate the unique characteristics of each distinguished professor, whereas the exercise is based on common characteristics and classifications.

The development of detailed criteria for the selection and promotion of faculty by rank and by department (with set weights for each criterion according to the salary equity analysis scheme in Exhibit 1) also is not suitable for direct application to the tenured faculty of major institutions. The primary criteria for appointment or promotion to tenure in major institutions are teaching and scholarship at the highest level. For different positions more weight may be put on one or another of those criteria but, as has been observed, completely separate consideration of each is incorrect as they are reinforcing and combine in human-capital building. A separate set of criteria for each department of the arts and sciences is generally considered unnecessary and undesirable.

A HEW request that a university "validate" all tests used in selection and promotion, if interpreted to cover faculty procedures, raises a host of serious questions. As indicated in the preceding footnote, Revised Order No. 4 contains such a requirement but it has not yet been widely applied to university faculty. As this is written in January 1974, a set of proposed regulations entitled "The Uniform Guidelines on Employee Selection Procedures" has been circulated for comment prior to publication in the *Federal Register* and application. The 27-page document, developed by the

Equal Employment Opportunity Coordinating Council of the federal government,[7] would not only regulate tests for aptitude and mechanical abilities but also any and all techniques used by employers to judge employees' relative qualifications for appointment and advancement. It is assumed in Washington that faculty appointments and promotions would come under the "uniform guidelines." That would involve government regulation enforced through insistence of "validation" of all means for judging the qualifications of teacher-scholars for particular openings. Those means include résumés stating one's educational credentials and record of work experience, scholarly publications, evaluations of applicants' published research results in professional reviews, systematic student evaluations of teaching, letters from prominent professors in a subfield giving their comparative evaluations of possible candidates, the unstructured interviewing of candidates, a lecture or seminar given by a candidate, etc. For each selection device, the burden of proof is placed on the federal contractor to prove lack of sex or race bias—no deviation from proportionality measured from some base. It is not clear how far HEW is asking Harvard to go into that thicket.

The salary equity analysis set forth in Exhibit 1 would, for faculty of major institutions, be quite unsatisfactory, and would be on a completely different basis from that used in enforcement of the equal-pay legislation. Essentially it is a crude six-factor analysis, with such gross data as "number of publications" and "number of committees"[8] on which the individual serves. As was explained in Chapter 3, use of 30 factors or variables in multiple-regression analysis to try to discover the extent of sex discrimination in faculty salaries is open to serious question and error. Years of faculty experience are subject to the differences that Johnson and Stafford's salary analysis demonstrates. For HEW to instruct Harvard to make salary equity analyses for women and minority persons according to the method and factors stated in Exhibit 1 indicates a

[7] The council agencies that drafted the document were the Office of Federal Contract Compliance of the Department of Labor, the Equal Employment Opportunity Commission, the Civil Rights Commission, the Civil Service Commission, and the Department of Justice.

[8] The inclusion of "number of committees" as one of the six factors is interesting. It is not included in the 30-odd variables used by Scott or Astin and Bayer. Among the requests to Harvard in HEW's letter of acceptance is a statement that "in line with the requirements of Revised Order No. 4," "each faculty" at Harvard should have an "affirmative action committee" with minority-group members and women who would "have a role in monitoring all appointments."

serious lack of understanding of the problem. Certainly it would be unsound to conclude that the "differential" so calculated "should be discriminatory."

The 10 items involve fundamental issues of administration and procedure. Yet Harvard was instructed as follows:

> We are aware of the necessary time constraints in developing satisfactory responses to each of the above items but would ask that a timetable be developed and submitted for each item detailing the proposed methodology for accomplishment of the task and the person or persons responsible. We will expect a response and commitment to the above within the next ten (10) days.

Obviously, those instructions assume no faculty participation in the decision with regard to the acceptance of items that could have a profound effect on faculty procedures and self-government. Within 10 days is hardly time for any serious consideration of such demands by the faculty of arts and sciences and the professional schools under the collegial system of shared responsibility.

AN IMPOSSIBLE TASK

In the midst of all this regulatory activity, the field staff of the HEW Office for Civil Rights has been given an almost impossible task. It is supposed to determine whether 916 colleges and universities, out of a total of approximately 2,500, are in compliance with Revised Order No. 4 and the HEW Guidelines. That is an average of about 16 institutions for each of the 58 field staff in the Higher Education Division of HEW's Office for Civil Rights.

The methods HEW uses for judging compliance or noncompliance are (1) on-site investigations, (2) negotiation with universities and approval or disapproval of their proposed affirmative action plans, (3) analysis of statistical reports and explanations from institutions, and (4) inquiries of the institution based on charges of discrimination affecting groups of employees, which are sent in to the regional offices from various sources. It is by such means that HEW's regional offices are supposed to determine whether the insitution is in compliance and whether it is using "good-faith efforts" to make an approved affirmative action plan work.

The HEW field staff generally do not have sufficient knowledge and experience to judge how appropriate numerical goals are for different academic departments in the arts and sciences in particular universities. They cannot be expected to know the demand and supply situation in each academic discipline in order to judge what numerical goals, if fulfilled, would or would not require reverse discrimination against white male faculty under the Civil Rights Act or equal-pay laws.

It is not surprising, therefore, that HEW "letters of findings" following on-site compliance reviews, or letters giving instructions with regard to substantive changes in proposed affirmative action plans, contain remarks that reveal lack of understanding of the way universities and faculty members operate. Also, it is not surprising that HEW refuses to accept responsibility for any action that a university takes in compliance with HEW Guidelines and an approved affirmative action plan.

The difficulties of the task assigned to the field staff are greatly enhanced by the deficiencies in the HEW Guidelines. Basic for reasonable and sensible enforcement with the kind of staff HEW can and will recruit is a less complicated and more suitable set of guidelines for affirmative action by universities and colleges. Proper guidelines for higher education would mean that university faculties at least, should no longer be regulated according to the provisions of Revised Order No. 4, which assumes the industry model of employment.

ONE REGULATORY STAFF FOR ALL MAJOR UNIVERSITIES

It is particularly inappropriate to have major universities divided among the regional offices for purposes of compliance review and determination of affirmative action requirements. Insistence that major institutions negotiate their numerical goals and administrative arrangements with the regional office staff, one at a time, is bound to mean unequal, inconsistent, and rather arbitrary treatment of universities, which are not regional but worldwide in reputation, drawing faculty and students from throughout the country and internationally.

To require the three or four dozen major universities to deal only with and through a regional staff is not sensible or appropriate for the following reasons: (1) four years of experience (1970 to 1974) have demonstrated that regional units vary widely in their understanding of how major universities operate, and need to operate, in their compliance practices and demands, and in the pace of their decision making; (2) the major universities compete nationwide for students and faculty (with significant numbers coming from abroad), they train most of the Ph.D. pool for the nation, and their faculties contain most of the outstanding teacher-scholars in the nation and are oriented to a considerable extent by discipline internationally; (3) the problems that major universities encounter under affirmative action and the contributions they can make to improve supply deficiencies of minority persons and women are similar and could be better handled by a cooperative approach on a national basis; (4) it is especially important to preserve the independence and effectiveness of the major universities because of the quality of their research and instructional contributions and their leadership in the academic world. There is need for HEW to explore the idea of joint planning for affirmative action with the major universities—planning on a cooperative basis for constructive purposes while recognizing institutional independence and differences.

It is unfortunate that certain HEW regional staff have insisted that one or more major universities conform to a certain set of affirmative action requirements, whereas directly competing institutions located in other regions, for a variety of personal and other reasons, have not been subjected to the same kind and intensity of federal regulation by HEW regional staff. Apparently, the regional offices have the power to reject proposed affirmative action plans but regional approval of a plan can be given only after Washington has approved the regional office's recommendation. By the time the regional office recommends approval to Washington, however, the regional staff has molded the plan in line with its views through the demands it has made and the negotiations it has carried on with the institution, sometimes backed by statements on what Washington will or will not approve.

National handling throughout by a single staff well versed in university operations would eliminate much of the arbitrary and inconsistent actions by regional offices and could help to develop a more constructive attitude and more intelligent programs. Single-staff handling of affirmative action plans for major universities is presented in Chapter 9 as part of a proposed program for government enforcement of nondiscrimination in faculty employment.

EXHIBIT 1: SALARY EQUITY ANALYSIS[9]

A salary equity analysis is required for all employees. The purpose of this is to determine whether or not employees engaged in similar work are paid different salaries due to their race and/or sex. To accomplish this it is necessary to determine if there is a salary differential and if that differential is actually the result of dis-

[9] This salary equity analysis is from "Attachment A" to a letter from John G. Bynoe, Regional Civil Rights Director, to President Derek C. Bok, Harvard University, dated Nov. 12, 1973, accepting Harvard's affirmative action plan.

criminatory practices rather than "bona fide" criteria. This analysis must be preceded by three (3) steps:

1 The development of detailed job position descriptions for each employee.

2 The validation of job position descriptions against the actual work performed by the employee or employees covered by the description.

3 The collecting of all job position descriptions into appropriate job classifications.

(These three (3) steps are covered in another part of this document.)

There are five (5) steps to accomplishing a salary equity analysis:

1 Establish all criteria relevant to a position.

2 Set weights on each criteria which reflect the relative importance of each criteria to the position. These weights should approximate as closely as possible the actual proportion of their values.

3 Do an aggregate comparison of white males and all females in each job position using names for each criteria and showing the means for annual salary increases and current salary

Show in this comparison the percent of the female mean to the male mean for each criteria and salary increases and current salary. Do the same type of comparison for majority group members and minority group members in each job position. Following is an example of this comparison for males and females.

EXAMPLE A

Criteria	*White Male*	*Female as % Male*	*All Female*
1. years at institution			
2. years in current job classification			
3. education level			
4. years of job-related experience			
5. number of publications			
6. number of committees			
Average annual salary increase			
Current Salary			

4 Validate the originally assigned weights according to the results of the aggregate comparisons for all white males in a position and adjust the weights accordingly to the final comparison. List criteria in descending order according to weight. These adjusted weights will appropriate the actual proportion of their values.

5 Compare each female to the white male with closest total weighting. Compare average annual salary increase and current salary. Do the same for each minority group member in each job position.

Female employees or minority employees with comparable weighed qualifications should have comparable salaries. If in the instance of equivalent standard point totals, the actual salaries are not equivalent, the differential should be considered discriminatory and the burden of proof shifts to the college to explain the differential. This must be explained in a narrative. Also, if the qualifications and standard value totals are similar but not equivalent, the system can be used to ascertain which portion of a difference in salary could be considered bona fide and which discriminatory.

8. *Government Regulation and University Effectiveness*

A university typically operates two different types of governing and personnel systems—one for faculty and the other for the supporting staff (clerical and administrative employees, food service personnel, grounds and building maintenance workers, and many others).

The faculty, or academic, system is characterized by collegial decision making by a community of scholars. It is basically democratic. Individual faculty in a department, school, and the university as a whole enjoy essentially the same professional rights and freedoms. In their teaching and research, most of them are fairly free from any direction and supervision by a management structure of authority.

For the most part, the supporting staff is subject to supervision and direction under a hierarchical authority system, similar to the governing arrangements in industry and in the administration of federal and state programs. In contrast to the largely democratic, self-directed system for faculty, the supporting staff is subject to a pyramid-type management exercised largely from the top down through a loose chain of command, with each level of operation under the supervision of, and subordinate to, the level above. It is understandable that many in the supporting staff of universities, and particularly professionals in research and library operations who consider themselves academics, have sought to achieve many of the privileges, freedoms, and self-governing advantages that faculty enjoy. Thus, features and practices of the faculty system have tended to spread into some nonfaculty areas, especially those where professional employees are in leadership positions.

Government programs of antidiscrimination enforcement have been designed and based on the industry-government model of personnel practice and authority. On bureaucratic grounds, rather uniform application of a regulatory program is generally considered essential for effective enforcement. University faculty are, of course, only a small fraction of the total coverage of such programs and generally constitute well under half of the university's own employment. Consequently, government compliance personnel, with backgrounds in business or government, cannot be expected to be interested in preserving and strengthening the faculty system of governance. Instead, as will be explained subsequently, through the rather inflexible application of rules designed for industry-model situations, their actions tend to weaken the faculty system and strengthen centralization of authority and control within the university. Thus, outside pressures are exerted in the name of antibias regulation that tend to undermine a system of work arrangements for faculty that nurtures independence of thought, creativity, and work satisfaction and has features that industrial relations specialists consider as part of the more meaningful and satisfying work life envisaged as a goal for industry in the future.

This chapter examines the implications of government regulation of universities under antibias enforcement based on the industry model. The faculty system will be discussed in terms of its significance for effective university operations and the problem of maintaining institutional integrity that arises with two different systems of governance and personnel practice in a university.

THE FACULTY SYSTEM AND INSTITUTIONAL INTEGRITY

As explained in Chapter 2, a university's reputation and contributions depend on the caliber of its faculty. The excellence of its faculty is likely, in considerable measure, to hinge on working arrangements that faculty find congenial and on rewards according to individual merit as judged by colleagues in the discipline.

The conditions that faculty in major universities consider ideal for their work satisfaction are in sharp contrast to the way business enterprises or government bureaucracies function. Distinguished faculty stress: (1) self-determination in their teaching and research, (2) departmental self-government through peer sharing of responsibility for the department's management and personnel decisions, and (3) professional evaluation of individual merit and performance, with reward according to such evaluation.

A large measure of professional responsibility for the staffing of academic departments is obviously necessary in major universities. It is unlikely that others in administrative positions (for example, the president, the provost, the deans, or the chairman of the university research board) would be competent to assess the comparative contributions that a distinguished scholar makes in his or her disciplinary specialty. They can, of course, and often do, participate in reviewing the documentation (including evaluations) submitted by a department in support of a proposed appointment or promotion.

The academic department, usually discipline-oriented, is the basic unit of organization in the arts and sciences. It is a loosely organized community with decisions made by collegial consent. There usually are no lines of authority within a department. The chairman, whose selection customarily involves consent of the professors in the department, is not in a superior or supervisory position compared with other faculty and may not enjoy as much intellectual authority in the department or the university as some other more academically prestigious members of the department. Also chairmanships are usually not held for more than two to five years, as teacher-scholars find that administrative duties cut into the heavy time-demands needed for maintaining distinction as a teacher and a scholar in a rapidly moving field. Because, in faculty matters, intellectual leadership rather than authority of position is important in decision making, HEW regional-office requests that universities include in their affirmative action plans an organization chart with lines of authority for faculty show a misconception of how faculty do and should function in major universities.

The collegial organization of department and university faculty provides each member with wide scope for individual initiative, for self-direction, and for professional creativity of a high order (Anderson, 1973). Academic freedoms, the academic work conditions, and the association with professional colleagues and able students serve to make a faculty career attractive to creative minds.

The nonacademic supporting staff has a regular scheduled work week, is directed by supervision during that period, and is subject to the discipline that goes with managerial authority. Selection among applicants for a nonacademic opening is usually made by one or more higher level administrators or academics serving in an administrative capacity. Supporting staff, except high-level administrators and professionals, are likely to be subject to many of the personnel practices in industry such as job descriptions, job evaluation, wage and salary administration, and performance appraisal by the supervisor. Nonacademic employees usually do not have tenure, paid leaves of absence for a term or an academic year, or vacation periods that amount to three or four months a year.

Many universities and colleges have sought to have certain items common to both faculty and supporting staff. For example, both may be covered by the same retirement, hospitalization, and other insurance programs. Dollar pools for annual wage and salary increases may be the same percentage of payroll for both, so that they have an identical average increase in percentage terms. However, the method of determining individual increases and the shape of their distribution statistically may be quite different.

The operation of two distinct systems of employment management and work life in a university can lead to misunderstanding and claims of apparent inconsistency and discrimination in status. The necessary differences between the two systems are not well understood and appreciated by government enforcement officials who lack academic experience. It is difficult, for example, for some government officials to appreciate that, with faculty, rank is based on individual qualifications and contributions and not job content and that a faculty member's job content usually does not change a bit with promotion to a higher rank. In contrast, promotion in industry and nonprofessional employment in the supporting staff of a university generally involves a change in job content—job levels and rates of pay are geared to the content or requirements of the job.[1]

The faculty compare work conditions, pay, and benefits with corresponding faculty in competing institutions throughout the country. For terms and conditions of employment and work management, most of the supporting staff generally are oriented toward corresponding work opportunities in industry in the local area for maintenance craftsmen, food-service workers, clerks and secretaries, and similar occupations.

The operation of two distinct systems of work management—one basically democratic and nationally oriented, the other mainly governed under hierarchal authority and locally oriented—can cause strains on grounds of unequal treatment and raise questions of institutional integrity.

[1] Edwin Young, chancellor of the University of Wisconsin at Madison points out that to tie faculty salaries to job descriptions and job content would "destroy" a major university's "ability to attract and reward the indispensable scholars and teachers." See Young (1973, p. 202).

Allegations of inequity and challenges to institutional integrity are stimulated by the existence of a third separate and different system for part-time student employment in the university, both in supporting services and as assistants to faculty in research. Generally, student employment is administered under student aid, so that it is not part of either the faculty or the supporting-staff employment systems. Hiring arrangements, pay levels, and record keeping for student work are usually handled separately from the other two systems.

In practice, personnel administration and management supervision are likely to be more mixed in character among supporting staff than the foregoing description may imply. Universities have been slow to adopt uniformly the systematic programs and techniques of personnel management found in most business corporations. Partly that has been because many of the supervisors of supporting staff are faculty who serve as chairmen of academic departments, academics who are directors of research programs or projects, and other professionally trained persons who perform supervisory functions as librarians, medical doctors, lawyers, architects, and electrical engineers running computer centers.

Both faculty and nonfaculty professionals are apt to be influenced in their thinking about management and personnel practices by the faculty system. In recent years there has been a definite movement on the part of some nonteaching professionals (for example, professional librarians and professional research staff) at universities to achieve more of the privileges and self-governing features of faculty life. Members of the professional research staffs have especially coveted the prestige and job security of faculty status. In addition, the development of university senates or councils composed of members selected from the administration, faculty, supporting staff, and students, who serve as part of the structure of university governance, is a further development toward participatory democracy for nonfaculty sections in the university.

Enforcement agencies (especially some HEW regional offices) and interest groups have put pressures on universities for uniformity of treatment for all employees. Through compliance reviews, complaints of discrimination filed with government agencies and the courts, and the threat of sizable liabilities under equal-pay laws, universities and colleges have been shocked into examining and improving their personnel policies and practices as applied to supporting staffs, especially from a legal viewpoint. The improvements have included good procedures for handling employee grievances and well-considered leave of absence arrangements. Unfortunately, government compliance officials may fail to appreciate that rules and practices suitable for the supporting-staff system of personnel management may not be appropriate for invariant application to the quite different work arrangements and work conditions for faculty.

GOVERNMENT PRESSURES ON THE FACULTY SYSTEM

Government agencies, through their directions, administrative rules, Executive orders, and oral and written inquiries and demands, try to move institutions of higher education toward the industry model in their academic operations. Government regulation is, for the most part, applied in a fairly uniform fashion to the two quite different systems of faculty and supporting staff.

The principal difficulties for universities with respect to faculty are (1) that HEW's administrative requirements for institutions restrict faculty self-determination and encourage pressures by minority and women interest groups, (2) that the federal government's increasing pressures for "validation" of faculty methods and techniques of selection[2] for faculty appointments and promotions calls into question the system of professional selection by mature teacher-scholars in a discipline and favors use only of methods that assure equality of results to be calculated on an uncertain base[3] and (3) that the application of equal-pay laws, which focus on the characteristics common to particular jobs rather than on the unique characteristics of individual teacher-scholars, tend to stress minimal qualifications for promotion and to undermine the merit system of faculty pay. Back of all these difficulties with government requirements is the underlying assumption that discrimination in employment will somehow disappear if only proportional representation for minority groups and women across the faculty board is forced on universities.

[2] As explained in the preceding chapter, validation for nonbias can be requested in connection with the use of any device or criterion (several are usually used together for screening purposes) such as résumés of education and experience, comparative evaluations by former teachers and leading scholars in the field, evaluation of the person's scholarly publications, student questionnaire evaluations of teaching in courses, results from interviewing the person, evaluations of a lecture or seminar given by a candidate.

[3] The persons to be included in the base or universe from which deviations from proportionality are to be calculated (total applicants for a position or only persons selected by some standard?) is usually unstated and unclear; this permits arbitrary application of the requirements. Total applicants could be a quite biased base.

The HEW Guidelines specify a required administrative arrangement for the implementation of an affirmative action program. An "executive," who "should be a person knowledgeable of and sensitive to the problems of women and minority groups," must be appointed "director" or "manager" of EEO programs. The establishment of one or more committees or task forces, "composed in substantial part of women and minority persons" is suggested to facilitate "the task of the EEO officer" and to enhance "the prospects of success for the affirmative action program in the institution."

The HEW Guidelines refer to Revised Order No. 4 for a statement of the activities and responsibilities of the EEO director. As stated there they include: development of "policy statements" and "affirmative action programs"; serving "as liaison between the contractor and enforcement agencies"; serving "as liaison between the contractor and minority organizations and community action groups concerned with employment opportunities of minorities and women"; having "active involvement with local minority organizations, women's organizations, community action groups and community service programs"; and reviewing "the qualifications of all employees to insure that minorities and women are given full opportunities for transfers and promotions."

Many universities have followed those instructions and suggestions, establishing a new position or positions in the office of the president, chancellor (provost), or both, and also establishing a universitywide committee or two (one for minority-group affairs and one for women's affairs) to aid the EEO officer (and the coordinator or director for women's affairs where there is such an office). In universities, persons appointed as EEO director or coordinator seem generally to be blacks or women. The EEO officer on his or her own authority, or with the support of the EEO committee, is likely to be able to influence recruitment procedures for faculty and supporting staff, to review actual recruitment in individual cases with respect to compliance, and to postpone or block action on a department's recommendation for a faculty appointment. It is understandable that a HEW regional office, in reviewing and negotiating with a university about a proposed affirmative action plan or developments under it, may be concerned with the actual authority that the EEO officer and/or the committee may have "to initiate and enforce remedies to problems or deficiencies." HEW seeks to have that person play a significant part in the compliance program.

In their capacity as liaison with HEW and other enforcement agencies, it may sometimes be unclear to what extent EEO officers are agents of the university and agents of HEW or other organizations. A black or female EEO officer can perform an important educational function within the university because of the experience he or she may bring to consideration of a problem or policy. However, insertion of another layer of administration with power to exercise a measure of influence and control over faculty appointments and promotions is likely to mean some restriction and restraint on the faculty system of professional evaluation and selection of faculty in a discipline and to result in additional centralization of power and control in the university.

Administrative pressures by HEW to make faculty selection and pay structures conform more closely to the industry model are also exerted through such means as (1) insistence that methods for the selection and promotion of faculty be validated on the basis of proportionality of results, (2) attempts under equal-pay enforcement to use job content rather than the individual's intellectual qualifications for specialized tenure positions in major universities, and (3) insistence that affirmative action numerical goals be calculated according to the prescribed method of an estimated labor market pool of qualified and available persons applied to all academic ranks and specialties. In such matters, HEW and other enforcement agencies have been prone to deny or disregard essential differences between the faculty system and the industry system.

The requirement that a university validate the selection methods used for faculty as well as supporting staff shows how the federal government may force the use of concepts from industry practice that are often ill-suited and of questionable validity when applied to faculty and faculty procedures. HEW compliance officials may insist that a university must, nevertheless, apply a test of proportionality of result to each element in the complex process of selection to fill a tenure opening by promotion from within or appointment from outside.

A part of federal effort to eliminate discrimination in employment is the provision that only elements proved not to have a biased impact on hiring and promotion can be used in selection for appointment or advancement. Sample surveys indicate that, due to affirmative action requirements and antidiscrimination legislation, a high proportion of business firms altered their selection criteria and revised their testing programs, changing or eliminating the use of preemployment tests and educational requirements that could not be closely related to performance on the particular job.[4]

As Chapter 2 explained, the criteria used in the selection of faculty—teaching, research, and other service to department and university—as applied to a particular professorship in a major university are likely to involve quite special and unusual qualifications, including a high degree of scholarly creativity. Consequently, university procedures place heavy reliance on the judgment of mature teacher-scholars in the discipline or subfield of the discipline, based on a variety of sources of information and evaluation.

The material used in the selection of a new faculty member would normally include: comparative analysis of the candidates' résumés showing their pertinent experience and accomplishments; letters from faculty in the field evaluating a candidate's relative standing and promise; student evaluations of various aspects of the individual's teaching in courses; critical reviews of the person's published and unpublished scholarly work; and conclusions of members of the department from personal interviews, from a class or seminar or lecture given on the campus, or from a paper delivered at a professional meeting. On the basis of such information and assessments, perhaps reviewed first by a search or screening committee that reports to the department, the tenured members of the department meet, discuss the relative merits of various candidates, and select a first choice and possibly a second one in case the top-ranking candidate rejects a proposed offer.

Evidently, it is practically impossible to validate in a formal manner each element in the procedure and the procedure as a whole, in order to prove that no part has a disproportionate impact on any group. Each item or source is designed to provide more complete information and to check on information or assessments from other sources. Elimination of the use of one or more sources because of an alleged disproportionate impact by sex, race, religion, or national origin would not be likely to lead to a more intelligent or objective result. Basically, a system of professional, peer-group analysis and selection involves reliance on the process if the procedures are properly followed and if those participating in the process are well qualified to make professional judgments in that field.

[4] See, for example, "Survey by BNA, ASPA Shows Impact of Equal Opportunity Requirements" (1973, especially p. C4). The sample consisted of 113 member firms of the American Society of Personnel Administration and was conducted by the Bureau of National Affairs.

Requests by compliance officers that standard tests used, say, in the selection of manual and clerical workers in a university's supporting staff be validated to make certain they contain no cultural or other bias are understandable as a part of enforcement of nondiscrimination in employment. The same is true of the requirement that a high school diploma is needed for the proper performance of low-level manual jobs.

However, a similar requirement for "validation" of the elements in the procedure for faculty selection and promotion may really involve a demand for radical change in the whole system of faculty selection. And it places in the hands of regional compliance officers a power of intrusion that can be quite arbitrarily applied one way to some institutions and rather differently, if at all, to others. Indeed, to require similar validation for faculty in major institutions is to question the very system of faculty self-determination.[5]

In a similar manner, the faculty system of compensation by relative merit, as determined by professional evaluation of individual performance and promise, is threatened by application of the concepts in the Equal Pay Act, which was extended to professional employees in mid-1972. That act requires the same rate of pay for men and women doing substantially similar tasks in the same place of employment. The act makes job content the controlling factor in determining compliance, and, thus, is difficult to apply to variations in the quality of intellectual performance and creativity.

Equal work is measured in terms of equal skill, equal effort, equal responsibility, and similar working conditions. These are all job traits. Again the government regulations with respect to sex discrimination are based on the industrial model, and are, therefore, ill-suited for faculty conditions and practice. As already explained, assistant, associate, and full professors may have the same job content in the department or in several departments. They may

[5] The HEW Guidelines (Office for Civil Rights, 1972, p. 10) refer to "the validation of all criteria for promotion." Revised Order No. 4 (par. 60-2.24*b*) states: "The contractor should validate worker specifications by division, department, location or other organizational unit and by job category using job performance criteria. Special attention should be given to academic experience and skill requirements to insure that the requirements in themselves do not constitute inadvertent discrimination. Specifications should be consistent for the same job classification in all locations and should be free from bias as regards to race, color, religion, sex, or national origin, except where sex is a bona fide occupational qualification. Where requirements screen out a disproportionate number of minorities or women such requirements should be professionally validated to job performance."

all teach at the same levels and be engaged in the same type of research. Their promotion from one rank to another is not based on a difference in job requirements so much as on the intellectual level of the teaching and research contribution and the corresponding academic reputation of the individual. The highest paid professor may be a person who has been in the same rank for 30 years. The base salary of department chairmen may be their regular salary as professors. On job-content grounds, professors of nuclear physics, economic theory, classics, and home economics might all seem required to have the same salary under equal-pay legislation.

Government regulation to eliminate sex discrimination in pay can result in a civil-service-like system of compensation for university faculty, with each rank defined in terms of minimum standards of skill, effort, and responsibility, and with specified pay grades within the rank through which the faculty member moves according to length of time in that rank or according to some other "objective" criterion.[6] In other words, application of equal-pay regulations can pose a threat to university methods and procedures for rewards and incentives for faculty.

The application of federal equal-pay legislation to university faculties raises another serious problem as a consequence of the demand for minority-group faculty stimulated by numerical goals in affirmative action plans. Many universities, in order to try to attract black faculty, have offered them salaries considerably above those for equally qualified white male and female faculty. Thus, in yielding to HEW pressures, those institutions have exposed themselves to a claim of unequal pay between some men and women. Under the law the women have grounds for lodging a formal complaint of sex discrimination, under which their pay would have to be brought up to the comparable level for black males. In turn, the white males could lodge a complaint of sex discrimination, under which their pay would be raised to that of white women.

Such a process is beginning to occur in certain institutions. It reveals the inconsistencies in the policies and in enforcement practice among different agencies of the federal government. Universities are being exposed to considerable cost for complying with the incompatible policies of government agencies under antibias legislation and contract compliance. It is understandable that university

[6] Sheldon E. Steinbach (1973, p. 52) points out such implications if present equal-pay regulations are applied to academic as opposed to nonacademic personnel. See also "Equal Pay in Higher Education . . ." (1973).

administrators and faculty are disturbed by confused signals from government in these matters.

THE PREDICAMENT OF UNIVERSITY ADMINISTRATORS

The application of government antibias programs to university faculty and supporting staffs has put many university presidents and top academic administrators in a difficult position. Generally they are—like most faculty—in full sympathy with the objectives of enlarging the opportunities for disadvantaged members of minorities and women to acquire adequate training for academic appointments, of expanding the scope of search for faculty, and of making the university's climate congenial for minority-group and female personnel. Most of them genuinely would like to be able to increase the minority-group and female component of the faculty.

A significant proportion of the presidents and top academic administrators have guilt feelings because studies have shown that some women in the faculty and supporting staff were being paid less than men for equivalent work. The central administration could be charged with condoning sex discrimination in such instances, because steps had not been taken earlier to eliminate such sex differentials, failure to do so being due perhaps to lack of attention and ignorance of the facts or to a belief that paying "the prevailing wage in the market" was a proper wage policy (Lester, 1948, pp. 13–17, 38–41).

With general charges of discrimination being made against most major institutions, university administrations and faculties moved to take corrective actions with respect to any proved discrimination among faculty or supporting staff. Corrective action was accelerated by pressures exerted by interest groups (in the student body, the faculty, the supporting staff, and outside organizations). Also, individual and class complaints were filed with federal and state agencies and the courts. Women's liberation was on the move, especially in the universities and colleges.

Some university administrators and faculty in 1972 and 1973 expressed concern that various pressures were being exerted on universities to force discrimination in favor of minority groups and women, to have institutions hire and promote some who were not the best qualified in order to rectify past race and sex discrimination. But top administrators of many universities, especially some large state institutions, were not in a strong position morally, politically, or legally to resist pressures for preference in hiring in view of past history, faculty and student opinion, the HEW Guidelines, and regional-office demands.

Morally, many university administrations and faculty were on the defensive. In some institutions, members of the faculty and/or supporting staff had received from their university "equity compensation" in response to their claims of sex discrimination or (rarely) race discrimination. In addition, the institution might seem to have admitted guilt when, according to government order, it calculated "deficiencies" and adopted numerical goals designed to eliminate those deficiencies. The invalid suppositions that underlie many calculated hiring goals have been fully explained in preceding chapters. Nevertheless the government scheme for hiring goals, by attributing all blame for sex and race disproportionality in a faculty to the demand side, puts university administrations and faculty under the burden of self-calculated sex and race bias.

University administrators were also in a weak public-relations position. Generally, they and their faculties favored federal action against race and sex discrimination in employment. It would have been difficult for them then to argue that antidiscrimination regulation under federal contracts was appropriate for industry but not for universities, or was possibly appropriate for the supporting staffs of universities but not for faculty, especially faculty of major institutions. That would leave them open to charges of elitism in a general climate of opinion favoring egalitarianism. Furthermore, the kind of analysis necessary to demonstrate the inappropriateness of numerical hiring goals for tenure faculty positions in distinguished universities or the inappropriateness of availability analysis and numerical goals with timetables, academic department by academic department, would be too complex and abstruse to be convincing to the general public.

Politically, the universities have also been in a weak position. They have found it difficult to take a strong, consistent stand, because the nature and timing of the impact of antidiscrimination enforcement has varied so widely among individual community colleges, four-year public colleges (some of which were former teachers colleges), four-year private colleges, and public and private universities. The associations of universities and colleges headquartered in Washington have, therefore, had trouble presenting a common front to the Nixon administration and Congress. With federal enforcement spread among four federal agencies (really 10 regional offices for HEW) and possibly between two state agencies (as well as the federal and state courts) and with enforcement action applied one institution at a time, the universities have been unable to marshal forces for more appropriate guidelines for governmental programs of antidiscrimination as applied to university faculty. In 1972 a number of university officials expressed to HEW and the Department of Labor strong opposition against any requirement of numerical goals with timetables for faculty, especially on a single-department basis. The HEW Guidelines of October 1972 seemed to recognize the persuasiveness of that presentation. As already explained, those guidelines state that a school, division, or a college "in many institutions" may be "the appropriate unit for goals." However, when Harvard in 1973 submitted an affirmative action plan, it was rejected by the regional office until Harvard capitulated and submitted a plan with numerical goals for each of its 30-odd departments of the arts and sciences faculty.

By the fall of 1973 a number of developments had increased the concern of universities with government enforcement programs and activities as they affect faculties and the opportunity of various groups for faculty employment. More universities and colleges were being pressed by HEW regional offices to comply strictly with the industrial-model requirements of Revised Order No. 4. The faculty system of professional evaluation for faculty appointments and promotions was being threatened by the proposed "Uniform Guidelines on Employee Selection Procedures."[7] Enforcement of equal-pay legislation was threatening to force some vulnerable universities to bring women's and then white males' pay up to the higher levels being paid to blacks. The inconsistencies between some regional enforcement of the HEW Guidelines and the race and sex blindness of the Civil Rights Act were threatening universities with suits charging discrimination against women and suits charging discrimination in favor of blacks and women. Some white males just acquiring Ph.D. degrees and some white male assistant professors pressing for promotion to tenure were complaining that their employment opportunities were being curtailed by preferences given to women and blacks. The EEOC was bringing an increasing number of court cases against universities for discrimination

[7] See p. 114.

against women, and some courts were using industry-model concepts in deciding faculty cases.

Given the weak political position of institutions of higher education, the outcome of such developments is difficult to predict. But it has become increasingly clear to university administrators that the only intelligent policy is consistently to follow the principle of equal employment opportunity—to have faculty appointed and promoted who, on the basis of their past performance, are judged by mature teacher-scholars to be the best available in terms of the requirements of the position. Also, that policy is consistent with the most effective pursuit of a university's educational goals.

Experience has demonstrated the need to work out a more intelligent and constructive program of affirmative action between government and universities. Such a program would involve more attention to the contribution that universities and government could cooperatively make to develop a larger supply of well-qualified women and minority persons for academic and other professional positions. Also there is need for some intelligent analysis of affirmative action and antibias enforcement on the demand side in the cases of universities. The next chapter deals with those subjects.

9. A Program for Enforcement of Nondiscrimination

This chapter sets forth a program for government enforcement of nondiscrimination in faculty employment that has been developed by the author. The program deals primarily with Executive order enforcement policy as applied by HEW.

One could argue that a comprehensive scheme of antibias regulation of universities, conducted by an administrative agency under Executive order, is not so necessary now that institutions of higher education are under the fairly comprehensive programs of antidiscrimination, involved in enforcing Title VII of the Civil Rights Act, the Equal Employment Opportunity Act of 1972, and the Equal Pay Act amendments of 1972 as well as state fair employment practices and equal-pay laws.

The program presented here assumes that properly formulated and properly enforced antidiscrimination guidelines under contract compliance could, on balance, provide sufficient positive benefits in terms of nondiscrimination in faculty employment to justify having such government regulation for several more years. In view of all the other antibias regulation of universities, however, the program under Executive order should be designed so that, at the appropriate time, it could be considerably contracted, if not completely terminated, with respect to university faculty.

Any program for Executive order enforcement as applied to faculty should be essentially in accord with the basic legislation for nondiscrimination in employment and pay as applied to faculty. Otherwise, a university's efforts to comply with all government agency directions and demands can only lead to inconsistent appointment and promotion decisions, which can expose the university to simultaneous charges of discrimination in favor of and against the same group, on grounds of race or sex.

The proposed program is designed to improve Executive order

enforcement of nondiscrimination in a number of respects: soundness of conceptions, consistency of policies, suitability for the special needs of higher education, avoidance of adverse effects on the educational objectives of institutions, restraint on the regulatory propensity for undue intrusion, and economy and efficiency of administration. In developing affirmative action guidelines, stress on those aims and considerations is important for gaining enlightened acceptance and pursuing intelligent enforcement.

This chapter first takes up the aims and considerations that experience indicates need stressing in a government program to enforce nondiscrimination in faculty employment under federal contract compliance. Next attention is given to the need for the government, as an important part of its compliance activity, to collect faculty data on a nationwide basis, covering projected and actual hirings, the terms of offers made, faculty movement among institutions, and individual charges of discrimination and their disposition. With timely data of that sort, the program could be monitored centrally, on a nationwide basis and for different segments of higher education. Analysis of the data could show the progress that is being made, the troublesome problems that are developing, and the revisions in the program that seem called for by experience.

Then, in the final section, the main elements in the proposed program are presented in fairly concise form. The program is designed primarily as a revision of the HEW Guidelines. It would also involve some changes in the jurisdiction or policies of other federal agencies, particularly in the Department of Labor. In addition, the voluntary program of private mediation-arbitration discussed in Chapter 6 is included as a significant element in the total program.

IMPORTANT CONSIDERATIONS IN DEVELOPING A PROGRAM

Experience is an acute teacher. Use of the HEW Guidelines for more than a year has taught both positive and negative lessons. We have learned which policies are appropriate and have desirable effects and which are ill-conceived and have unfortunate consequences. Much has also been learned about the administration of government antibias programs that seek to enforce nondiscrimination and various kinds of "affirmative action."

1 Guidelines for affirmative action plans should be based on a knowledge of the facts, a well-considered formulation of objectives, clear

definitions and concepts, appropriate analytical methods, and arrangements for intelligent, sensible enforcement.

Higher education guidelines designed to apply to faculty should be geared to the special, rather unique systems for hiring and promotion for teacher-scholars, particularly at major universities. Therefore, guidelines for the antibias regulation of university faculty should be conceptually and administratively distinct from those for industry or for the nonacademic, supporting staffs of universities. Revised Order No. 4 as presently conceived and applied is inappropriate for application to most tenure faculty positions in major institutions. The facts of academic life, including specialization by a subfield of a discipline and considerable differences in abilities and competencies among experienced teacher-scholars in a subfield, make highly questionable any attempt to apply unsophisticated notions of availability, utilization, deficiency, proportionality, and numerical goals with timetables to faculty positions beyond those to be filled by new Ph.D's beginning their teaching-research careers.

2 All parts of the federal effort to achieve nondiscrimination in higher education should be consistent in aim and policy. Federal authorities should be clear and in agreement with respect to proper policies:

(a) To rectify past discrimination in individual and class cases and prevent such discrimination in the future

(b) To correct university policies (for example, employee benefits, leaves for childbearing and child-rearing, part-time tenure appointments, antinepotism rules) that may operate in a discriminatory fashion

(c) To prevent new discrimination in hiring, promotion, or compensation

A set of federal guidelines that results in inflated numerical goals and stimulates pressures for preferential hiring and promotion by race and sex serves to increase the amount of discrimination,[1] which is inconsistent with the provisions of federal legislation and the stated aims of federal agencies. Guidelines for higher education should be clear of purpose and consistent in practice with respect to those matters.

Given the very special features of the faculty system of appointment and promotion, a strong case can be made for a single federal

[1] Preferential hiring and preference in promotion discriminate for some groups and against others, thus adding to the amount of discrimination, as Daniel Seligman (1973) points out.

regulatory agency for antibias enforcement, at least for the faculties of institutions of higher education. It may not be possible to have the necessary consistency of enforcement goals, policy, procedure, and data requirements if enforcement is parceled out to four or more different federal agencies (HEW, the Office of Contract Compliance and the Wage-Hour Division of the Employment Standards Administration in the U.S. Department of Labor, and the Equal Employment Opportunity Commission plus the Civil Rights Commission and the Department of Justice).

3 Under the affirmative action plans of major universities, stress should be placed on, and ample credit given for, developing a larger supply of female and minority-group faculty qualified for tenure appointment at high-ranking institutions. Such accomplishment could constitute the most significant affirmative action contribution that some major universities could make toward equalizing the chances of female and minority-group faculty to achieve high-level appointments. The working out, under government regulation, of incentives and credits for the appropriate recruiting and training of graduate students and assistant professors prior to a tenure appointment would present some practical problems, which are treated below.

4 The importance of intellectual autonomy for universities should be recognized and care should be taken to avoid, as much as possible, any detailed regulation of their internal operations. That includes forgoing efforts to restructure and redistribute authority and actions that would increase the centralization of power and authority in the university at the expense of faculty self-government and professional assessment of faculty qualifications. Care should be taken to avoid, through federal regulation, a weakening or displacement of the faculty system of professional decision making on faculty staffing by insistence on the application to faculty of personnel-management techniques based on an industrial model. Unintelligent, dysfunctional regulation along those lines is likely to hamper universities in the most effective pursuit of their educational and research goals over the long run.

5 In the enforcement of equal opportunity for all faculty, due recognition should be given to the primacy of the basic objectives—the mission—of a major university, namely:

(a) The discovery of important new knowledge

(b) The cultivation, through faculty instruction, of an understanding of

existing knowledge, the ability to use that knowledge, and the competence to develop new knowledge

(c) The training of students in professional schools in the understanding and practice of a systematic body of specialized knowledge

Care should be taken that government regulations and enforcement demands do not adversely affect a university's ability to pursue those basic objectives. It should be recognized that the quality of mind of the faculty member, of his or her faculty colleagues, and of the students (as well as the academic atmosphere and opportunities in the department and the institution) affect the quality of the results achieved through both teaching and research.

Those five points or considerations should be carefully taken into account in framing and enforcing federal guidelines for nondiscrimination and appropriate affirmative action at institutions of higher education. The program presented below has been designed with them firmly in mind.

ROLE OF DATA COLLECTION AND ANALYSIS

Proper reporting by all universities and colleges covered by HEW regulation could provide the basis for the development and operation of a more intelligent, equitable, effective, and economical program of federal antibias regulation of institutions of higher education than the present one. Comparative analyses of the faculty data so collected would help the federal government to monitor the program on a nationwide basis and by separate parts of higher education as well as by individual institution.

For the most part the reports from individual institutions would supply quantitative data, accompanied by explanations for certain figures. More descriptive would be reports on recruitment efforts and complaints. Comparative analyses of both quantitative and qualitative material in reports would enable government analysts to draw general conclusions on the mismatch between demand and supply by discipline and subfield, broken down by race and sex for assistant professor positions and tenure openings. Such analyses could be used to draw conclusions about the extent and nature of discrimination against or in favor of different races and sexes, in different disciplines, in different categories of institutions, and in different regions.

The kinds of data and information that would be most helpful to collect and analyze for program and enforcement purposes (including leads for field investigations) are the following:

1 Each institution would be required to report each July the numerical hiring goals for the nontenure ranks in its affirmative action plan, by race and sex for the succeeding two years.

2 Each institution would report each January its faculty hires and terminations for the previous six months (July to December), and each July its faculty hires and terminations for the preceding six months' period from January through June, giving the salary and rank offered to each new minority person or woman hired and the salary and rank for each nonminority male hired. For the same periods, all faculty terminations would be reported with a brief comment concerning each termination.

3 Each institution would report each year in July the number of faculty in each department (and professional school) by rank, broken down by race and sex, who were employed on May 1.[2]

4 Each institution that grants an average of 10 or more Ph.D.'s a year would report in June each year *(a)* the number of such degrees granted by department, broken down by race and sex, and *(b)* the experience in placing its Ph.D. candidates and recipients in academic positions outside the institution.

5 Each institution should gather and maintain in one office a full record of the recruitment efforts, the selection process, and the offer or offers made for each faculty opening.[3] In that way the material would be well organized and readily available for examination by compliance officials checking on the compliance of that institution with respect to faculty hiring.

6 Each institution should report to HEW[4] whenever a faculty member (or applicant for a faculty position) lodges a complaint of discrimination in employment against the institution with a federal or state agency or a court, giving the essentials of the allegation. HEW would arrange for reporting by other federal agencies of faculty complaints of discrimination in employment filed with them.

[2] Salary is not asked for existing employees as it is for new hires, because comparisons of salary figures, apart from a knowledge of individual qualifications and experience, are not very meaningful or informative, especially where the numbers are too small (particularly for minority persons and women by rank in most departments) to calculate statistically valid averages for comparison by sex and race.

[3] A form for organizing such material could be adopted by the federal government for use by the institutions.

[4] This assumes that HEW would be the central agency for antibias regulation of institutions of higher education.

The institutions would report to HEW periodically with respect to progress in settlement of each case and its final disposition.

7 HEW would add up the projected nontenure hiring goals in affirmative action plans by race and sex and the total nontenure hires by race and sex for the same period, and compare and analyze them by category of institution. HEW would also analyze for faculty the terminations by race and sex and type of institution, and the terms of offers made and accepted by persons coming from a regular faculty position in another institution.

8 HEW would classify and analyze individual complaint data to determine the incidence of such complaints, the experience with their settlement, and the implications of the data and experience for government antibias programs and for enforcement policies and practices.

Such a set of reports and their analysis would have a number of advantages from the point of view of intelligent operation of the program and equity in the functioning of compliance review and analysis. A systematic program for data reporting would put all covered institutions on a par in terms of reporting requirements, timing of a review of their data, and analysis of their relative standing and rate of progress.

The preparation and findings of periodic reports can stimulate thought and discussion concerning the institution's efforts and relative position, by the administration, faculty, and others in the university community. No university or college will have reason to lack concern because of apparent neglect by HEW. Without such a reporting system, it will be years before HEW makes any significant contact with all of some 900 universities and colleges, or even half of them, that it covers.

Such systematic reporting would facilitate intelligent and objective selecting and scheduling of institutions for field investigation. Comparative analysis of submitted data, and not such factors as nearness to the regional office or militancy of particular advocacy groups, would provide the basis for determining the timing and frequency of HEW field investigations at particular institutions. The collection and analysis of such comparable data should also serve to reduce the time spent by HEW staff in field investigation.

Such a system of periodic data reports might seem to place a heavy burden on colleges and universities. If the other federal agencies could work out with HEW a standard form for such data that would meet the needs of all of them, and perhaps the state agencies as well, that would reduce the time university personnel spend on separate, uncoordinated reports in connection with antibias regulation. Also, lessening the time spent by university administrators and faculty with field investigations would mean added saving for the institutions. On net balance, such a data reporting system could prove economical for most institutions.

The chief benefit provided by such data and analyses of them would be a better factual basis for guiding administration of the program, for drawing conclusions about the impact of the program, and for making appropriate revisions and improvements in the program and its enforcement.

ESSENTIALS OF AN APPROPRIATE, EFFECTIVE PROGRAM

This section presents the substance of a positive program for both the development of larger numbers of highly qualified female and minority-group faculty and the enforcement of equal opportunity in faculty employment, with major universities especially in mind. In developing this program, attention has been given to the five considerations discussed earlier in this chapter, and the program assumes that a data-reporting system such as the one just outlined is in operation.

First, the main components or features of the program are presented in outline form. They are six in number. The reasoning or basis of support for those components has, for the most part, been given in the preceding chapters. For some elements or aspects further elaboration may, however, be needed. Such elaboration is presented sequentially after the outline statement of the six components, which follows.

1 An affirmative action program for increasing the supply of highly qualified female and minority-group teacher-scholars in certain academic disciplines and fields of professional practice where the supply of teacher-researchers is exceedingly thin. The mechanism for developing much larger numbers of supply qualified for high-level faculty appointments in selected fields is competitive submission of "affirmative action supply programs" by universities for HEW selection and approval. The plans would provide for unrestricted selection by the university of those female and minority-group applicants to participate in that university's program for supply development. (This proposal is explained in some detail in an appendix to this chapter.)

2 Use of availability-utilization analysis and numerical goals to achieve "proportionality" to be confined to first regular appointments of new and prospective Ph.D. holders to the position of assistant professor or advanced instructor on the ladder of professional advancement. Thus, "affirmative action demand plans" would be focused on those who are at the same stage of career development, namely, recent completion or practical completion of Ph.D. requirements.

3 For enforcement of nondiscrimination for faculty appointments other than first appointment as assistant professor and for promotions within the professorial ranks, use of *(a)* analysis of data in the periodic reports of institutions, *(b)* field examination of the institution's central file of information on each faculty appointment and promotion, *(c)* the procedures for settling individual faculty complaints of discrimination, including the system of mediation-arbitration presented in Chapter 6, *(d)* the Equal Employment Opportunity Commission and state agencies for antidiscrimination enforcement, and *(e)* the courts.

4 Concentration in a single agency (HEW) of the administrative oversight of affirmative action plans and compliance, as applied to faculty (including professional research staffs) in higher education. That would mean removing faculty of colleges and universities from the Department of Labor's jurisdiction for contract compliance and, thus, from the provisions of Revised Order No. 4. Supporting staffs generally would, on the other hand, remain under Revised Order No. 4 as long as it applies to similar operations and occupations in industry.

5 HEW regulation for the faculty of major universities and other institutions that recruit a majority of their faculty in the national market to be handled by one well-qualified unit instead of ten regional offices. That would mean central handling of such faculty with respect to affirmative action supply plans and affirmative action demand plans, data analysis, and compliance enforcement.

6 A restructuring and strengthening of the staff of the Higher Education Division of the Office for Civil Rights in HEW, so that it is suited to meet the added responsibilities and functions to be placed upon it, especially the central unit to handle major universities and other institutions recruiting nationally, and to analyze the data reports.

Much of the factual background and the analytical bases for the six main components of the proposed program have been discussed in Chapters 2 through 8. Nevertheless, it may be helpful to comment briefly on each of the six and their interrelationships.

1 Failure to take account of the supply aspects in developing affirmative action plans and the need to increase the supply of women and minority persons qualified for appointments as tenured faculty were pointed out in Chapters 3 and 5. Experience in this country and abroad, particularly Russia, clearly indicates the need for vigorous, well-supported efforts to develop a critical mass of women and blacks qualified for tenure appointments in the natural sciences and engineering. Such faculty supply is needed to teach graduate courses and do research in disciplines that have a bearing on problems such as energy, pollution, and transportation, so that female and minority-group researchers would be attracted into and trained for work in those areas. Without special efforts on the supply side, experience and data show that the development of a proper supply will be a slow and lengthy process.

A specific proposal for increasing significantly the supply of female and black faculty well qualified for tenure appointments in fields where their supply is quite thin is spelled out in some detail in the appendix to this chapter. The proposal involves universities submitting affirmative action supply (AAS) plans, from which HEW would select the needed numbers for approval. The AAS plans would be for graduate training for the Ph.D. degree and postdoctoral training as teacher-scholars while on assistant professor appointments. It is suggested that the fields for such a breakthrough action on the supply side might include, in the arts and sciences, the disciplines of chemistry, economics, geology, mathematics, physics, and statistics, and among the professional schools: architecture and urban planning, business administration, engineering, and public administration.

As is explained in the appendix, an approved affirmative action supply plan would be taken into account favorably in considering a university's whole program for equal employment opportunity for faculty. It would be necessary to protect the process of selection by a university of graduate students and assistant professors for participation under an AAS plan from vulnerability to charges of discrimination against white males on account of their exclusion from a plan's purview. The university would still be subject to nondiscrimination requirements—under legislation and contract compliance—for all faculty employment not included in approved AAS plans. The AAS plans would not involve government control over faculty selection of female and minority-group graduate students and junior faculty to participate in such plans nor would they give cause for any regulation that would tend to alter or weaken faculty self-government and the faculty's role in selection and promotion of faculty.

2 The grounds for the proposal to confine availability-utilization analysis and numerical goals based on that type of analysis to the first regular appointment as assistant professor (or advanced instructor) were fully explained in Chapter 4. Chapters 3 and 4 also explained why supply and demand conditions for tenure positions at major universities were generally inappropriate for such availability-utilization analysis and for numerical goals based on such analysis.

3 The third component deals with the detection and determination of noncompliance and discrimination in faculty employment, especially for areas where the method of utilization analysis and numerical goals is inappropriate and leads to erroneous conclusions. It suggests reliance, in part, on the kinds of data analysis discussed earlier in this chapter. The results of such analysis should assist in the selection of institutions and areas for questioning and further examination, including field investigation if necessary.

Individual complaints can be an effective method of enforcement, especially if nondiscrimination or the elimination of demand discrimination, and not calculated numerical goals, is the compliance objective.

The purpose in establishing a faculty complaint procedure and in proposing the system of mediation-arbitration by experienced outside faculty in Chapter 6 was to facilitate prompt submission of faculty complaints of discrimination and to have them settled intelligently and correctly—by private settlement within the faculty system if possible. In addition, complaint can be made directly to federal and state antidiscrimination agencies and the courts.

HEW personnel are prone to overstress numerical goals and to underestimate the enforcement power of individual complaints, especially by faculty who enjoy certain customary and legal protections growing out of faculty status. That may be because HEW itself had so much difficulty and was relatively ineffective in handling individual complaints of discrimination and "reverse discrimination" that were filed prior to mid-1972, when individual complaints of discrimination against institutions of higher education were transferred to the Equal Employment Opportunity Commission.

4 The advantages to both the government and the institutions of having a single agency collect the data and administer the various aspects of affirmative action and antidiscrimination for faculty (except for individual complaints filed with federal and state agencies under the Civil Rights Act and state antidiscrimination legislation and legal actions handled by the Justice Department) should be obvious. Federal antibias regulation for faculty could be administered much more consistently, intelligently, and economically. Responsibility for planning, administering programs, and conducting enforcement activities would be in the hands of one agency, which should consequently have knowledgeable and qualified staff. The institutions of higher education would have one agency to deal with and one set of comprehensive reports to make, thus reducing confusion, frustration, and cost. A set of relationships could be developed between that agency and the institutions of higher education that would be constructive and effective in promoting mutual interests and goals.

5 The grounds for proposing that a single administrative unit within HEW handle faculty of major universities were explained in the last section of Chapter 7. With central collection and analysis of data and with enforcement activities partly based on such analysis, a good case can be made for single administrative handling of the faculty of universities and colleges that recruit the bulk of their faculty in a national market. Admittedly there could be practical difficulties in drawing a line between institutions on that basis. Nevertheless a strong argument can be made for national handling of at least faculty recruitment, initial appointment, and interinstitutional movement in connection with new appointments, in the case of those institutions that compete largely in the national market for faculty.

6 Chapter 7 explained the need for increasing the qualifications of the staff of the Higher Education Division of HEW, especially with respect to knowledge of and experience in the faculty systems of recruitment, appointment, and promotion, particularly in major universities. Assuming the adoption of all or most of the previous

five components, the need for bringing to the staff more knowledgeable and analytically qualified personnel is all the greater. In dealing with programs and regulations to apply to faculty, mutual understanding and respect contribute to constructive solutions.

These six components of a program are presented here, not as a completely finished product but as basic elements for discussion and a foundation for the development of a federal program for assuring equal employment opportunity and nondiscrimination in faculties of institutions of higher learning, while at the same time not decreasing, but hopefully increasing, the effectiveness of their instructional and research programs.

Obviously, the legal and practical aspects of such a program would need to be given much more detailed consideration.[5] With respect to constitutional questions, it should be pointed out that the proposal for affirmative action supply plans differs significantly from the present program of affirmative action plans on the demand side under the HEW Guidelines. The latter program is applied uniformly to all institutions of higher education with federal contracts. Therefore, it encompasses the bulk of the market for university faculty.

The program of affirmative action supply plans, on the other hand, would apply only to selected fields in selected institutions, and then only to a part of the graduate students or junior faculty in those fields at those institutions. In the case of graduate-student AAS plans, it could well be that the numbers would simply be added to the institution's regular complement of graduate students so that no displacement would be involved. Even if there were some displacement at that institution, the opportunity for male white graduate students to obtain excellent graduate instruction would be restricted to only a small extent in view of the large numbers of universities that would be offering graduate instruction without an approved AAS plan in those fields.

The impact of AAS plans for nontenure faculty positions might be more significant because the possibility of expansion in number

[5] It is possible, for example, that the following provision of Title IX of the Higher Education Amendments of 1972 would need to be amended if federal fellowships were to be provided for graduate students under AAS plans: "No person in the United States shall, on the basis of sex, be excluded from participation in, be denied the benefits of, or be subjected to discrimination under any education program or activity receiving Federal financial assistance."

of faculty at a particular institution is likely to be less than for graduate students. That difference could be reduced by an expansion of government contracts that would increase research opportunities in the discipline at that institution. In any case, the restricted areas of faculty employment under AAS plans would be in specified fields and for only a part of the nontenured faculty employment —usually much less than half—in the field or fields at that institution. Again, in view of the large number of universities without AAS plans, the overall restriction on opportunities for nontenured faculty employment for white males would be small. That is especially the case in view of the fact those fields were selected because they have few female and minority-group faculty throughout the nation.

The proposed AAS plans further illustrate how government antidiscrimination plans can, by intelligent planning and working with universities on specific problems, avoid detailed intervention in the internal operations of universities.

The next chapter discusses the role that academic leadership might play in moving forward the kind of program presented in this chapter.

APPENDIX TO CHAPTER 9: Proposal for Affirmative Action on the Supply Side

This is an elaboration of the first component of the proposed program discussed in the last section of Chapter 9, pages 146–147.

Purpose This proposal is designed to increase significantly the supply of female and minority-group faculty who are qualified for university positions carrying tenure in fields where they have heretofore been quite rare. The aim would be to develop enough women and minority persons as outstanding teacher-scholars to provide a critical mass, and thus to eliminate a sense of peculiarity, separateness, and other restraints on the development and use of their talents for such a career. By providing a critical mass, the proposal would hope to reduce subtle barriers and to provide the momentum for further increases after the government's affirmative supply effort in that field is discontinued.

Fields for supply development Criteria for the selection of fields for such supply development would include: (1) the scarcity of female and/or minority-group senior faculty in the field and (2) the relative need for talented female and minority-group teacher-scholars in the field to help train female and minority-group practitioners and teacher-scholars for the future. Among the fields that should be considered in the arts and sciences are chemistry, economics, geology, mathematics, physics, and statistics; and among the professional schools: architecture and urban planning, business administration, engineering, and public administration.

Kinds of training and development For increasing the supply of well-qualified female and minority-group faculty in a selected field, government encouragement and support would be needed for the two stages of advanced training and development: (1) graduate training for the Ph.D. or its equivalent and (2) postdoctoral development as a teacher-scholar during the first five to seven years as a regular faculty member, when one needs the opportunities to make a reputation as a teacher-researcher that would qualify him or her for a tenure post at a respected institution of higher education.

The duration of graduate training for the Ph.D. might be considered four years. The development period as assistant professor is usually five to seven years. Together they amount to about ten years but, of course, each stage could be handled separately. What these time intervals do indicate is the rather long training period to achieve prominence as a teacher-scholar.

Encouragement of affirmative action supply plans The federal government, after selecting the fields for such special supply-increase efforts and deciding for each field the increase in numbers it wishes at each stage each year, would establish the terms of encouragement and support that such plans would have. To help attract female and minority-group Ph.D. candidates into those fields and to demonstrate the federal government's interest in doing so, probably some federal support for fellowships would be needed in addition to university and possibly foundation fellowship funds. That would also provide some incentive for universities to submit affirmative action supply plans for Ph.D. training.

For teacher-scholar development of assistant professors, probably no federal financial support would be necessary. The individuals selected would be paid regular salaries for regular faculty service. Universities would presumably be interested in submitting AAS plans for such reasons as the following: (1) the institution's faculty and administration have a genuine desire to expand the number of highly qualified female and minority-group faculty in the field, (2) credit would be given to such an effort in terms of contract compliance, and (3) the numbers of female and/or minority-group assistant professors in an AAS plan would displace the numerical goals for such assistant professors in the institution's affirmative action demand plan, and such goals would be difficult to work out for those fields in any case. Furthermore, it would be necessary to recognize that female and/or minority-group assistant professors recruited under plans for supply increase would not be likely to have the same opportunities for promotion to tenure at their institution as assistant professors appointed on the basis of open competition, with the prospects for a tenure opening more definitely in mind. Those differences should, however, in no way preclude promotion of assistant professors appointed under a supply-increase plan, if that is warranted in open competition, or perhaps inviting them back at a later date. Those possibilities could be among the potential benefits of the plan for the institution.

Content of AAS plans The federal government would specify the material that should be submitted by institutions in the competition to obtain government approval for an AAS plan for Ph.D. training, for the development of able and effective teacher-scholars, or both. An institution's graduate-student AAS plan would specify by year the number of female and minority-group graduate students to be in Ph.D. training under the plan. An institution's faculty-development AAS plan would specify the number of female and/or minority-group assistant professors (and advanced instructors where that is the initial appointment) to be on the faculty each year.

In a graduate student plan, the institution would describe its Ph.D. degree requirements and the nature and content of its graduate training in the field, including the quality of the faculty, the research training facilities and opportunities for graduate students, the quality and numbers of graduate students, the average length of time to complete Ph.D. requirements, the record of the institution's Ph.D. recipients later as teacher-scholars, and similar data.

In the faculty-development plan, the institution would need to set forth the opportunities for its assistant professors to achieve outstanding records in teaching and research. The pertinent material would include: teaching opportunities in undergraduate and graduate courses, teaching loads, quality of students, paid and unpaid leaves of absence for research, research opportunities and support, library and computer facilities, quality of tenured and nontenured faculty, opportunities for discussion with tenured faculty concerning professional matters, and other aspects of teaching and research at the institution. Assurance would need to be given that assistant professors under the AAS plan would have the same rights, privileges, and opportunities as other assistant professors.

Under an accepted AAS plan the university would be free to recruit and select female and minority-group graduate students and junior faculty according to the institution's (faculty and deans) judgment of the persons best qualified for its graduate training or assistant professor teaching and research, from among the candidates it is able to recruit. In other words, the institutions would retain freedom of selection of graduate students and junior faculty, and the students and Ph.D. holders seeking assistant professorships would have freedom of choice of university.

Selection and oversight of AAS plans The federal government, in deciding which among the AAS plans submitted it will accept, would base the decision mainly on the quality of the instruction in that field at that institution in the case of graduate-training AAS plans and on the opportunities for developing into outstanding teacher-scholars there in the case of faculty AAS plans.

Government oversight of the accepted plans would be confined to ascertaining whether the institution was performing according to the provisions of its plan as officially accepted. Judgment on that score could be based largely on written reports. Failure to comply with its accepted plan, if not corrected, could lead to withdrawal of acceptance, along with the attendant government support and privileges.

10. *Academic Leadership and Constructive Action*

The preceding chapters have presented an analysis of the federal government's program of antibias regulation as it is being applied to the faculties of universities. They have shown that the federal program has been flawed by some misconceptions, inappropriate methods of analysis, and erroneous conclusions based on faulty analysis. The main defects in the program can be summarized as follows:

1. Failure to recognize and take into account the fact that demand for tenured faculty is highly individualistic and selective, based on personal achievement of the highest quality as a teacher-scholar and stimulated by competition for excellence of faculty (Chapter 2)
2. Failure to make a proper analysis of supply differences by sex and race for academic disciplines and subfields, and to take special account, in affirmative action plans, of human-capital development on the job during the five to seven years after receipt of the Ph.D. degree (Chapter 3)
3. Flaws in the conception and measurement of discrimination under availability-utilization analysis that result in placing undue blame and remedial responsibility on the demand side and lead to inflated numerical hiring goals (Chapters 4 and 5)
4. Pressures for discriminatory hiring to meet inflated goals, resulting in additional, new discrimination and the likelihood of an increasing number of "mistakes" in the selection of tenured faculty (Chapters 2, 3, and 5)
5. Government application of the industry model of authority and personnel management to university faculty operations, with the consequent threat to the faculty system of collegial decision making based on professional assessment of merit (Chapters 7 and 8)

6 Increasingly involved and intrusive regulation of faculty decision making, with the negotiation and enforcement of each successive affirmative action plan (Chapters 7 and 8)

7 Inconsistent government policies and regulatory treatment between government agencies and different HEW field offices, opening up added legal liabilities for universities and affecting arbitrarily and unevenly their ability to compete for faculty, students, and resources, nationwide and internationally (Chapters 4 and 6)

Those seven defects characterize the federal regulatory system as applied to universities and colleges generally. They are defects from the viewpoint of most of the 900-odd universities and colleges covered by the HEW system of antibias regulation. HEW's mistaken assumptions and policies are likely to be about as inappropriate for nonmajor institutions of higher education as they are for major universities.

Indeed, the particular interests of the nonmajors are likely to receive even less consideration by the HEW regional offices because they are not in as strong a position to resist singly the regulatory program of HEW. Patterns of affirmative action plans are being set by HEW regional-office negotiations with the major universities. Those patterns are not likely to take adequate account of the needs and special interests of different types of nonmajor institutions.

Generally speaking, a less prestigious institution will find it difficult to effectively resist pattern spreading negotiated by the one-institution-at-a-time enforcement tactic. Under that tactic, the other categories of institutions are not in a good position to press for needed and appropriate reform of the HEW regulatory system from their viewpoint.

RESPONSIBILITIES OF THE ACADEMIC COMMUNITY

If the programs of government regulation of universities and colleges for antidiscrimination purposes are to be intelligently formulated and properly applied, the faculties and administrations of universities need to consider the difficulties and implications of the present programs. For a variety of reasons, a surprising amount of ignorance exists among university faculty concerning the actual demands that HEW regional offices are making and the far-reaching implications that they and court cases can have for the future of higher education in this country.

Analysis of difficulties and defects of existing antibias enforcement can point the way to more appropriate solutions. Painful experience with adversary contests in agency hearings and the courts encouraged the development of the limited mediation-arbitration proposal for individual complaints of discrimination by faculty members in Chapter 6. It is a procedure for constructive settlement within the university community.

The fairly comprehensive program for government enforcement of equal opportunity for faculty proposed in the preceding chapter is designed especially to meet serious objections to and defects in the existing government programs of antibias enforcement in higher education.

Clearly in a matter as subtle and complicated as discrimination in employment in university faculty, one program cannot be expected to satisfy all the needs and concerns of the various interested parties. Although feelings of sex, race, or religious prejudice cannot be fully eliminated from university faculties, strenuous efforts must be made to assure equal opportunity to all to excel, and to avoid any adverse effects of such bias on the professional careers of individuals.

Some may consider the program set forth in Chapter 9 to be too attentive to the concerns and objectives of the leading universities—"the elite" of higher education. The analysis of government antibias regulation in this book has dealt with problems particularly of those institutions for three reasons: (1) HEW's mistaken assumptions concerning qualified supply and numerical hiring goals are very clear, and the potential for lasting injury to the nation's preeminent instructional and research resources is so evident, in the case of the leading institutions, (2) the world of higher education looks to the major universities for much of the leadership, especially in faculty matters, and (3) HEW appears to have chosen many of the prominent universities to achieve breakthroughs and pattern setting in government regulation of university faculty.[1]

The faculties and administrations of universities and colleges in other classifications could suggest additions or complementary

[1] In the letter stating the HEW found MIT's affirmative action plan "acceptable and in substantial compliance," the regional civil rights director noted that in some respects MIT had gone beyond minimum standards of compliance and was the first institution of higher education in Region I to work out with HEW numerical goals by academic department. With respect to such pattern setting, the director said: "We'll be able to help a lot of universities as a result of what you've done." (*Tech Talk*, 1973*b*, p. 1). Help has taken the form of HEW insistence that Harvard and other major institutions in Region I must have numerical goals by individual department in the arts and sciences.

features to the Chapter 9 program, needed to fit their circumstances. It is important that faculty members and administrators in various types of institutions consider the kind of government regulation that suits both the goal of equal employment opportunity and their particular needs.

Some in academia may argue that parts or all of HEW's program of affirmative action should be abandoned either as impractical or inappropriate and uncorrectable. For reasons presented at various points in these pages, abandonment of the affirmative action part of federal contract compliance at this stage of development would seem to be premature.

The case for excluding university and college faculty from coverage under the Equal Pay Act is more persuasive. That legislation uses "job content" as the basis for determining sex equity in the wage and salary structure at a particular location. That concept simply does not fit long-established promotion and salary-setting practices for university and college faculty. To bend universities' systems of salary and salary-increase determination to fit concepts of the Equal Pay Law could practically destroy their effectiveness.

University administrators may find it awkward and retrogressive—even elitist—to have different government regulatory programs and agencies for faculty and for supporting staff. It can be argued that the appointment of a new financial vice-president, a librarian, a director of admissions, or a personnel director for a university can involve individual supply aspects and search and selection processes not very different from those that apply in the selection of a professor of classical Greek philosophy, high-energy physics, or microeconomic theory. Distinguished professors in particular subfields may be more rare, but search for the best-qualified person for a top nonfaculty post in a particular university setting may demonstrate that the notion of a qualified pool does not fit that situation very well either.

Clearly, however, the answer is not that individual faculty should be treated differently because they are personally so different or somehow better than individual members of supporting staffs. It is that the system of teacher-scholar training, faculty operation, and selection for tenure posts is basically different, and that the differences are too important for effective operation of universities to have them obliterated by a common program of government regulation that is applied in a strictly conformist fashion. Undoubtedly in many universities, professionals on the supporting staff, such as professional researchers with Ph.D. degrees and perhaps professional librarians, should be included under a regulatory program for faculty.

The specifics of antibias regulation of universities and colleges should be carefully analyzed and thoroughly discussed, both on the campus and in Washington. Reform should be based on facts and experience, and on long-range planning as well as short-run concerns.

The faculties and administrations of universities have an obligation to provide intelligent leadership with respect to antibias regulation of higher education in this country. They have a large stake in the faculty system of professional evaluation of qualifications and responsibility for academic affairs. Universities have gained much of their strength and effectiveness from that faculty system, and should be prepared to take affirmative action to preserve and advance its values.

THE FACULTY SYSTEM UNDER PRESSURE

During the next five years, the faculty system of appointment and advancement according to professional judgment of individual merit will be under considerable pressure.

In the five academic years of 1969–70 through 1973–74 many blacks and women were appointed as assistant professors in university faculties. In a number of cases, they enjoyed some advantage or preference in connection with their initial appointment. Some risks were taken. During the next five years, most of those assistant professors will become subject to a decision on either promotion to tenure or termination of appointment.

HEW-enforced hiring and promotion goals have generated a new set of pressures. They, of course, are designed to increase the number of female and minority-group appointments in each department according to timetables under many affirmative action plans. However, any preferential treatment in promotion or appointment to tenure on grounds of race or sex would be likely to violate Title VII of the Civil Rights Act and could expose the university involved to heavy costs, including the possibility of duplicate tenure appointments for a single opening under a court decision.

The demand-supply situation is another complicating factor. The leveling off of demand for faculty—overall stability in faculty positions and openings since 1970—has created in most disciplines a condition of general oversupply of persons with Ph.D. degrees desiring academic appointment. The quality of available supply is generally better than it was five or ten years ago. Thus, supply crowding exists and will continue to exist with respect to tenure appointments.

Over the years, various criticisms have been made of the system of faculty assessment of qualifications for appointment and promotion. Most of the criticism has been generated by cases that involved a negative decision on an assistant professor's promotion to tenure. As explained in Chapter 2, even in periods of faculty expansion and a more balanced demand-supply situation, only a fraction of all assistant professors were promoted to tenure at many major universities.

Campus criticisms and lessons learned from past mistakes have often resulted in improvements in the process of information gathering, in the quality and objectivity of evaluations, or in faculty procedures to assure due process. Also, a university's system of faculty selection is being tested constantly as offers are made to faculty at other institutions, as faculty move between universities, and as the results of decisions on promotion to tenure are reviewed. The long tenure period that individual faculty have makes it difficult for department members to overlook the lessons of past misjudgments.

Persons in academic life have exceptional opportunities to make individual reputations as teacher-scholars. Their qualities as a teacher become known through their students, departmental colleagues, oral presentations at professional meetings and seminars at other universities, and the textbooks they write. Their research contributions are made available for professional evaluation through articles in scholarly and scientific journals and through published books. In short, university faculty have the advantages of a large number of potential employers, many outlets for the presentation of their scholarly contributions, and a variety of sources for judgments of their work; they can literally teach and write their way to the top in open competition.

Although those opportunities for career advancement provide individuals considerable protection against the impediments of prejudice, they are less effective in a slack market for those who are not in the very top level of accomplishment and for those who are tied to a particular location. A married woman may, for example, need to pursue her academic career within a particular local institution.

University faculty and administrators should be in a position to defend the fairness of the faculty selection and promotion system at their institutions. Therefore, such systems should be examined in terms of the following questions:

- How well are the system's rationale and its actual operation understood by both nontenured and tenured faculty?[2]
- Are the procedures well designed to bring up for consideration those teacher-scholars from whom the best possible candidate for the position can be selected?
- Are the criteria and methods of assessing the merits of several alternative candidates well designed to lead to appointment of the one best qualified for the post?
- Is the information on the leading candidates to be used as the basis for department action as thorough and accurate as possible?
- Does the procedure provide for evaluation of the leading candidates' qualifications for the position by professionals well suited for that purpose, including outside distinguished scholars where external assessment would contribute to the making of an intelligent decision?
- Does the procedure provide for adequate consideration of the documentary information and evaluations prior to department action, with opportunity for individual members of the department to submit separate statements to the administration expressing their views?
- Does the procedure provide that a department recommendation for tenure appointment by promotion or appointment from outside (as well as a negative decision on promotion to tenure that requires termination) is subject to broader review by a committee composed of (say) members elected from the university or college faculty, selected faculty members and academic administrators, or a combination of distinguished scholars from outside and within the university?

[2] For material explaining the aims and operation of particular systems of faculty selection and promotion, see *A Report of the University of Chicago . . .* (1972) and *An Information Statement for the Guidance of New Faculty at Princeton University* (1972). For a discussion of criteria, materials, procedures, and practices for tenure appointments at Harvard, see *Discussion Memorandum on Academic Tenure at Harvard* (1971), especially pp. 21–27, and Appendix B, "Preparation of Materials for Ad Hoc Committees on Permanent Appointments in the Faculty of Arts and Sciences," pp. 36–40.

The aim in filling a tenure post presumably is to appoint the candidate who, in that post, would make the greatest contribution to the educational objectives of that university. An assistant professor on the ground whose performance in teaching, scholarship, and general advancement of the intellectual life on the campus have been outstanding would tend to have an inside track on a tenure opening if one developed that just suited his or her abilities, training, and academic interests. A major university should generally apply the same standards for tenure appointments whether candidates are from within or outside. However, distinguished performance in that university's setting should provide a fairly firm basis for predicting the quality of the individual's future achievement. For that reason, mature teacher-scholars in the discipline would be inclined to favor a candidate with proven local experience.

There is a need to make certain that each assistant professor understands the application of the system to his or her case and does not develop unrealistic expectations concerning prospects for promotion to tenure at that university. One way to accomplish those purposes is to have the department chairman, at least once a year, discuss with each assistant professor in the department individually his or her performance as a teacher, researcher, and colleague, and the assistant professor's prospects for a tenure appointment at that university. The chairman's statements should be based on a discussion with the tenured professors concerning each assistant professor and the likelihood of the development of a tenure opening in the right subfield during the limited period one can hold an assistant professorship. Such a department discussion can appropriately be held in connection with the annual salary review in institutions where department faculty of higher rank make department recommendations on individual salary increases on the basis of merit.

The vital importance of distinguished appointments to the tenured faculty of a major university is well stated by the Committee on the Criteria of Academic Appointment of the University of Chicago as follows:

> The function of appointive bodies is to bring to the academic staff of the University individuals who will perform at the highest level the functions of research, teaching, and training and the maintenance of the intellectual community of the Universtiy. A university which does not perform at this level will lose its standing in the world and therewith its power to attract outstanding faculty members and outstanding students. Its failure to at-

tract them will in turn reduce the quality of its performance. Every appointment of a mediocre candidate makes it more difficult to appoint a distinguished candidate later and makes it more difficult to bring outstanding students to the University. This is why scrupulous insistence on the most demanding criteria in the act of appointment is so decisive for the University (*A Report of the University of Chicago . . .*, 1972).

CONCERN AND OPPORTUNITY

The continuing drive of talented women and members of minorities to excel in the arts and sciences and in professional careers presents the universities and the nation with a magnificent opportunity. That momentum, flowering under equal opportunity, can over time greatly enrich professional talent in this country and especially in university faculties in various disciplines.

It would be unfortunate, indeed, if inept regulation, promoting discrimination under a dual standard, should discredit the program. The university community has a responsibility to save the HEW antibias program from that fate.

The faculties and administrations of universities must work for the adoption of suitable and constructive programs, by the institutions and the government, to assure equal employment opportunity for members of minorities and women in the faculties of universities. Basic facts and considerations that need to be taken into account in designing antiprejudice programs of faculty appointment and advancement have been set forth above. Hopefully, the analysis and proposals offered in these pages will stimulate appropriate "affirmative action" on the part of leadership elements in academia and in government.

References

"Affirmative Action in Higher Education: A Report by the Council Commission on Discrimination," *AAUP Bulletin,* vol. 59, pp. 178–183, Summer 1973.[1]

Alexander v. Gardner-Denver Co., 42 LW 4214 (1974).

Anderson, G. Lester: "Bureaucracy, Idiosyncrasy, Tolerability, and Academic Personnel Administration," *Journal of College and University Personnel Administration,* vol. 4, pp. 33–35, September 1973.

Astin, Helen S.: *The Woman Doctorate in America: Origins, Career, and Family,* Russell Sage Foundation, New York, 1969.

Astin, Helen S., and Alan E. Bayer: "Sex Discrimination in Academe," in A. S. Rossi and A. Calderwood (eds.), *Academic Women on the Move,* Russell Sage Foundation, New York, 1973.

Bayer, Alan E.: *College and University Faculty: A Statistical Description,* ACE research reports, vol. 5, no. 5, American Council on Education, Washington, D.C., June 1970.

Bayer, Alan E.: *Teaching Faculty in Academe: 1972–73,* ACE research reports, vol. 8, no. 2, American Council on Education, Washington, D.C., August 1973.

Ben-David, Joseph: *American Higher Education: Directions Old and New,* McGraw-Hill Book Company, New York, 1972.

Bickel, Alexander M.: Brief of Anti-Defamation League of B'nai B'rith as *Amicus Curiae* in Support of Jurisdictional Statement or in the Alternative Petition for Certiorari, *Marco De Funis et al. v. Charles Odegaard,* President of the University of Washington et al., Supreme Court of the United States, October Term 1973, no. 73-235.

Bowen, William G., and T. Aldrich Finegan: *The Economics of Labor Force Participation,* Princeton University Press, Princeton, N.J., 1969.

[1] The use of the term *Commission* in the title appears to be in error.

Brewster, Kingman: "On Tenure," *AAUP Bulletin,* vol. 58, pp. 381–383, Winter 1972.

Bryant, James W.: *A Survey of Black American Doctorates,* Ford Foundation, New York, 1969.

Bunzel, John H.: "The Quota Mentality," *Freedom at Issue,* no. 22, pp. 10–14, November–December 1973.

Carnegie Commission on Higher Education: *A Classification of Institutions of Higher Education,* Berkeley, Calif., 1973*a*.

Carnegie Commission on Higher Education: *Opportunities for Women in Higher Education: Their Current Participation, Prospects for the Future, and Recommendations for Action,* McGraw-Hill Book Company, New York, 1973*b*.

Cole, Stephen, and Jonathan R. Cole: "Scientific Output and Recognition: A Study in the Operation of the Reward System in Science," *American Sociological Review,* vol. 32, pp. 377–390, June 1967.

Commission on Academic Tenure in Higher Education: *Faculty Tenure,* Jossey-Bass Inc., Publishers, San Francisco, 1973.

Daily Labor Report, no. 34, pp. E1-E8, Feb. 19, 1974.

Discussion Memorandum on Academic Tenure at Harvard University, Cambridge Committee on Governance, Harvard University, Cambridge, Mass., November 1971.

Dodge, Norton T.: *Women in the Soviet Economy: Their Role in Economic, Scientific, and Technical Development,* Johns Hopkins Press, Baltimore, 1966.

"Equal Pay in Higher Education Highlights Discussion at ESA Meeting," *Daily Labor Report,* no. 24, pp. A9–A10, Dec. 14, 1973.

Federal Register, Oct. 2, 1971*a* and Dec. 4, 1971*b*.

Galbraith, J. K., E. Kuh, and L. C. Thurow: "The Galbraith Plan to Promote the Minorities," *New York Times Magazine,* Aug. 22, 1971, pp. 9, 35, 38, 40.

Galenson, Marjorie: *Women and Work: An International Comparison,* New York State School of Industrial and Labor Relations, Cornell University, Ithaca, N.Y., 1973.

Griggs v. Duke Power Co., 401 U.S. 424 (1971).

Harvard University Gazette, vol. 69, p. 8, Nov. 16, 1973.

An Information Statement for the Guidance of New Faculty at Princeton University, Office of the Dean of the Faculty, Princeton University, Princeton, N.J., October 1972.

Johnson, George E., and Frank P. Stafford: "The Earnings and Promotion of Women Faculty," *American Economic Review,* forthcoming.

Kerr, Clark: "Foreword," in Dael Wolfle, *The Home of Science: The Role of the University,* McGraw-Hill Book Company, New York, 1972.

Ladd, Everett C. , Jr. , and Seymour M. Lipset: *Academics, Politics, and the 1972 Election,* American Enterprise Institute for Public Policy Research, Washington, D.C., 1973.

Lester, Richard A.: *Company Wage Policy: A Survey of Patterns and Experience,* Industrial Relations Section, Princeton University, Princeton, N.J., 1948.

Lester, Richard A.: *Hiring Practices and Labor Competition,* Industrial Relations Section, Princeton University, Princeton, N.J., 1954.

Malkiel, Burton J., and Judith A. Malkiel: "Male-Female Pay Differentials in Professional Employment," *American Economic Review,* vol. 63, pp. 693–705, September 1973.

Merton, Robert K., and Harriet Zuckerman: "Institutionalized Patterns of Evaluation in Science," in R. Merton, *The Sociology of Science: Theoretical and Empirical Investigations,* University of Chicago Press, Chicago, 1973, pp. 460–496. Also published as "Patterns of Evaluation in Science: Institutionalisation, Structure and Function of the Referree System," *Minerva,* vol. 9, pp. 66–100, January 1971.

Mommsen, Kent G.: "Black Ph.D.'s in the American Marketplace: Supply, Demand, and Price," *Journal of Higher Education,* forthcoming.

Mooney, Joseph D.: "Attrition among Ph.D. Candidates: An Analysis of a Cohort of Recent Woodrow Wilson Fellows," *Journal of Human Resources,* vol. 3, pp. 47–62, Winter 1968.

National Academy of Sciences: *Careers of Ph.D.'s: Academic versus Nonacademic,* Washington, D.C., 1968.

National Science Foundation: *American Scientific Manpower: 1970—A Report of the National Register of Scientific and Technical Personnel,* Washington, D.C., 1971.

New York Times, p. 37, Feb. 29, 1972.

Office for Civil Rights, U.S. Department of Health, Education, and Welfare: *Higher Education Guidelines,* Washington, D.C., Oct. 1, 1972.

Office of Equal Employment Opportunity Programs, New York: *Equal Employment Opportunity in the State University of New York,* Albany, N.Y., Dec. 1, 1972.

President's Commission on the Status of Women: *American Women,* Washington, D.C., Oct. 11, 1963.

Rafky, David M.: "The Black Academic in the Marketplace," *Change,* vol. 3, pp. 6, 65, 66, October 1971.

A Report of the University of Chicago Committee on the Criteria of Academic Appointment, University of Chicago, Chicago, Ill., 1972, reprinted from *The University of Chicago Record,* vol. 4, December 1970, and vol. 6, January 1972.

Seligman, Daniel: "How 'Equal Opportunity' Turned into Employment Quotas," *Fortune,* vol. 87, pp. 166–168, March 1973.

Sherain, Howard: "The Questionable Legality of Affirmative Action," *Journal of Urban Law,* vol. 51, pp. 25–47, August 1973.

Simon, Rita James, Shirley Merritt Clark, and Kathleen Galway: "The Women Ph.D.: A Recent Profile," *Social Problems,* vol. 15, Fall 1967.

Statement of the Anti-Defamation League of B'nai B'rith, submitted to the New York State Advisory Committee to the U.S. Commission on Civil Rights for inclusion in the Hearing in Albany on June 6 and 7, 1973.

Steinbach, Sheldon E.: "Fighting Campus Job Discrimination," *Change,* vol. 5, pp. 51–52, November 1973.

"Survey by BNA, ASPA Shows Impact of Equal Opportunity Requirements," *Daily Labor Report,* no. 240, pp. C1–C9, Dec. 13, 1973.

"Surviving the Seventies: Report on the Economic Status of the Profession, 1972–73," part IV, "The AAUP Sponsored Study of Determinants of Salary Differentials," *AAUP Bulletin,* vol. 59, pp. 203–205, Summer 1973.

Tech Talk, Massachusetts Institute of Technology, vol. 18, Apr. 11, 1973*a.* and July 25, 1973*b.*

"The Threat of Inflationary Erosion: The Annual Report on the Economic Status of the Profession, 1968–69," *AAUP Bulletin,* vol. 55, pp. 192–253, Summer 1969.

Weitzman, Lenore J.: "Affirmative Action Plans for Eliminating Sex Discrimination in Academe," in A. S. Rossi and A. Calderwood (eds.), *Academic Women on the Move,* Russell Sage Foundation, New York, 1973.

Young, Edwin: "Personnel Relations in Non-Profit Institutions," in Gerald E. Somers (ed.), *The Next Twenty-Five Years of Industrial Relations,* Industrial Relations Research Association, Madison, Wis., 1973, p. 202.